SUBSTANCE ABUSE COUNSELORS

PRACTICAL CAREER GUIDES

Series Editor: Kezia Endsley

SUBSTANCE ABUSE COUNSELORS

A Practical Career Guide

TRACY BROWN HAMILTON

ROWMAN & LITTLEFIELD
Lanham • Boulder • New York • London

Published by Rowman & Littlefield
An imprint of The Rowman & Littlefield Publishing Group, Inc.
4501 Forbes Boulevard, Suite 200, Lanham, Maryland 20706
www.rowman.com

6 Tinworth Street, London, SE11 5AL, United Kingdom

British Library Cataloguing in Publication Information Available

Library of Congress Cataloging-in-Publication Data

Names: Hamilton, Tracy Brown, author.
Title: Substance abuse counselors : a practical career guide / Tracy Brown Hamilton.
Description: Lanham : Rowman & Littlefield, [2021] | Series: Practical career guides | Includes bibliographical references. | Summary: "Substance Abuse Counselors: A Practical Career Guide will help you determine if this is the right career for you and what skills and educational background you need to succeed in this field, and it includes interviews with substance abuse counselors currently working in the field."—Provided by publisher.
Identifiers: LCCN 2021020118 (print) | LCCN 2021020119 (ebook) | ISBN 9781538159224 (paperback) | ISBN 9781538159231 (epub)
Subjects: LCSH: Social work with drug addicts. | Drug addicts—Counseling of. | Vocational guidance.
Classification: LCC HV5825 .H2144 2021 (print) | LCC HV5825 (ebook) | DDC 362.29/186—dc23
LC record available at https://lccn.loc.gov/2021020118
LC ebook record available at https://lccn.loc.gov/2021020119

Contents

Introduction

So You Want a Career as a Substance Abuse Counselor?

*T*hat you have picked up and begun reading this book means you are considering pursuing a career as a substance abuse counselor. This likely means you are interested in helping people to overcome a dependency on a substance, be it alcohol, a narcotic, or other drug, to guide them in getting back on track with their health, relationships, and careers. Perhaps you have experience with substance abuse yourself or have known someone to suffer an addiction. Regardless of your reasons, reading this book is a positive first step in understanding the role of a substance abuse counselor, what kind of education and experience the field requires, and most importantly, whether this is the right career choice for you.

According to *Merriam-Webster*, substance abuse refers to the "excessive use of a drug (such as alcohol, narcotics, or cocaine)" or "use of a drug without medical justification."[1] An addict is defined as "one exhibiting a compulsive, chronic, physiological or psychological need for a habit-forming substance, behavior, or activity."[2] Substance abuse counselors apply their training to helping addicts or substance abusers overcome their dependence.

Problems with addiction have far-reaching consequences that affect not only the health, safety, and well-being of an individual but also those close to the person. Addiction can destroy trust and break relationships with families, friends, and coworkers. And it's a more common problem than you might think. The following statistics were published in 2020:[3]

- Almost 21 million Americans have at least one addiction, yet only 10 percent of them receive treatment.
- Drug overdose deaths have more than tripled since 1990.
- From 1999 to 2017, more than 700,000 Americans died from overdosing on a drug.

- Alcohol and drug addiction cost the US economy more than $600 billion every year.
- In 2017, 34.2 million Americans committed driving under the influence (DUI), 21.4 million under the influence of alcohol, and 12.8 million under the influence of drugs.
- About 20 percent of Americans who have depression or an anxiety disorder also have a substance use disorder.
- More than 90 percent of people who have an addiction started to drink alcohol or use drugs before they were eighteen years old.
- Americans between the ages of eighteen and twenty-five are most likely to use addictive drugs.

But the positive news is that many addicts are able to recover and turn their lives around—and beginning a life of recovery often comes with the guidance and support of a substance abuse counselor, which is a big part of what makes this career choice such a satisfying one. Counselors can work with groups or focus more intensely one-on-one with clients.

Being a substance abuse counselor gives you the opportunity to help individuals overcome their addictions and put them on a path to repairing their lives and their physical and mental health. With this as the goal, a substance abuse counselor works with clients to:

- Diagnose and assess problems with addiction and substance abuse.
- Identify issues relating to addiction problems and determine goals.
- Decide on a treatment plan and approach.
- Refer clients to various support groups to reinforce treatment.
- Lead therapy sessions, both group and individual.
- Help clients find a job or career to ensure stability.
- Update reports for the courts as needed.
- Meet with family members for support and for additional guidance.
- Arrange medical interventions if needed and provide longer-term addiction management support.

This book is the ideal start for understanding the role of a substance abuse counselor, the various environments in which substance abuse counselors work, and the path that should be followed to ensure you have all the training, education, and experience needed to succeed in your future career goals.

It will also help you understand how to begin now, whether you are a middle-school or high school student or a university graduate, to set yourself on the course to a successful career as a substance abuse counselor.

A Career as a Substance Abuse Counselor

Substance abuse counselors are different from doctors or psychologists. They do not prescribe medication or provide psychological therapy. Instead, they focus on practical issues, such as helping a client gain employment to achieve stability—including financial stability—in their lives. Substance abuse counselors work in a variety of environments, including group homes where addicts stay while in recovery, hospitals, prisons, treatment centers, or private practices. This book will cover the various work environments and the specific tasks substance abuse counselors fulfill in their role.

NOTE: The ongoing coronavirus disease (COVID-19) pandemic has seen a rise in opioid and other substance abuse problems,[4] as people struggle with the isolation of lockdowns and working or studying from home. At the same time, because of social-distancing precautions, many people have not been able to seek in-patient counseling in the traditional way. Counselors have also had to adjust how they work with clients, with many having to adapt to online, virtual counseling sessions.

Substance abuse counselors hold degrees in counseling or a related field (all of which will be discussed later in the book) and also must earn certifications to practice legally. Many substance abuse counselors also contribute to research in the areas of addiction treatments and recovery methods.

The Market Today

How does the job market look for young people seeking to work as substance abuse counselors? It's actually a fast-growing field, making it a smart career choice.

"When you are working with someone, trying to get them un-stuck, over the speed bump they're faced with on their life's journey, and something clicks for them, that feels like magic. Helping people understand how and why they have emotions, and what the heck to do with them when they are there, is incredibly satisfying."— Michelle Hominick Anderson, registered social worker and addiction counselor

According to the US Bureau of Labor Statistics (BLS),[5] employment for substance abuse counselors—as well as behavioral disorder and health counselors—is projected to grow a strong 25 percent between 2019 and 2029. This is a far greater rate of growth than average for an occupation. This is a positive projection, both for those in the substance abuse counseling profession and for those seeking help with substance abuse problems.

Becoming a substance abuse counselor gives you the opportunity to have a positive and direct impact on the lives, health, well-being, and relationships of people struggling with substance abuse issues or addiction.
Halfpoint/iStock/Getty Images

What Does This Book Cover?

This book covers the following topics relating to substance abuse counselor careers:

- Understanding what substance abuse counselors do and what characteristics many who land in these fields possess.
- How to form a career plan—starting now, wherever you are in your education—and how to start taking the steps that will best lead to success.
- Educational requirements and opportunities and how to fulfill them.
- Tips on writing your résumé, interviewing, networking, and applying for jobs.
- Resources for further information.

Where Do You Start?

As this book will show, no matter where you are in your education, from junior high to college graduate and beyond, it is never too soon to get started pursuing a career in substance abuse counseling. Whether you are keeping up with the latest treatment approaches through reading books and journals or brushing up on related skills in classes offered at your college or high school, you can start your career preparation now.

Once you've read this book, you will be well on your way to understanding what kind of career you want, what you can expect from it, and how to go about planning and beginning your path.

Let's get started.

Why Choose a Career as a Substance Abuse Counselor?

*A*re you a good listener and reliable confidant? Are you nonjudgmental with a genuine interest in helping people overcome their struggles and live happier, healthier lives, with fulfilling careers and stable relationships? Are you interested in how the mind works and in mental health in general? Do you have personal experience with substance abuse, be it your own experience or that of someone close to you? There are many reasons why a career as a substance abuse counselor appeals to people; these are just a few.

The fact that you picked this book off the shelves and are reading it indicates that you are considering substance abuse counseling as a career. Choosing a career is a difficult task, but as we discuss in more detail in chapter 2, there are many methods and means of support to help you refine your career goal and focus on a profession that will be satisfying and will fit you and your natural characteristics and interests the best.

Of course, the first step is understanding what a particular field—in this case, substance abuse counseling—actually encompasses and informing yourself of the future outlook of the profession. That is the emphasis of this chapter, which looks at defining the field in general and then in more specific terms, as well as examining the past and predicted future of the field.

As with any career, there are pros and cons, which we will discuss. In balancing the good points and less attractive points of a career, you must ask yourself whether, in the end, the positive outweighs any negatives you may discover. This chapter will also help you decide if a career in substance abuse counseling is actually the right choice for you. And if you decide it is, the next chapter will further offer suggestions for how to prepare your career path, including questions to ask yourself and resources to help you determine more specifically what kind of career related to substance abuse counseling suits you best.

Different Types of Substance Abuse Therapies

As mentioned in the introduction, substance abuse counselors work in various environments. They can work in schools, prisons, treatment facilities, or hospitals. They can work in a private practice or for the government. They can focus on particular groups, such as veterans, the homeless, or teenagers.

There are just as many treatment types and approaches as there are types of substance abusers and types of substances that can be abused.[1] Although when thinking about addiction or substance abuse treatments, many people may imagine group meetings taking place in public spaces such as church basements or libraries—such as Alcohol Anonymous or Narcotics Anonymous gatherings—but these types of therapies and support groups are not right for everyone.

Researchers in counseling techniques and related subjects are constantly looking for new, innovative ways to help people with substance abuse problems overcome their addictions and set about repairing the damages caused by their reliance on alcohol or another drug. This entails identifying and addressing the core of the problem, the circumstances or events that contributed to the abuse of a substance in the first place, such as a traumatic experience, stress, or loss, so that a person can overcome destructive patterns and begin to heal. There are also some genetic and environmental conditions that can make a person more prone to substance abuse than others. Finding treatment that works relies on identifying and understanding the causes and how best to combat them.

Some of these treatment methods require additional training or certification before a counselor can practice them with clients. What follows is an overview of common therapies and practices used to help people struggling with substance abuse problems.

BEHAVIORAL THERAPIES

So-called behavioral therapies focus on guiding a client to understand the root causes of destructive, high-risk behaviors. There are several forms of therapy that fall under the category of behavioral therapy.

- Cognitive behavioral therapy (CBT): Found to be effective with cases of alcohol, marijuana, cocaine, methamphetamine, and nicotine addiction, CBT helps clients anticipate situations that are high risk, meaning that tend to prompt the desire to abuse a substance. Through CBT, a person learns to apply strategies—including avoidance and self-control—to avoid relapse. This centers on identifying "triggers" that lead to substance abuse.

- Dialectical behavior therapy (DBT): This type of therapy has been shown to be effective against self-destructive behaviors, including substance abuse, but also behaviors such as eating and personality disorders. DBT focuses on relaxation practices such as yoga and controlled-breathing exercises to help improve focus and calm and to strengthen a client's ability to deal with negative thoughts without resorting to destructive behaviors.
- The Matrix model: Primarily used with clients suffering addiction to methamphetamine or cocaine, the Matrix model provides a framework for long-term abstinence from drug use. The method involves a counselor working as a coach, developing a trusting relationship with the client, and promoting self-worth and encouraging group and family therapy. The method also entails drug testing.

EYE MOVEMENT DESENSITIZATION AND REPROCESSING (EMDR)

Many substance abuse problems are triggered by a traumatic event that a person struggles to move beyond and, therefore, develops a dependence on a substance to function, which, of course, creates more problems. EMDR therapy helps a person reprocess a memory of a traumatizing event so its negative impact can be reduced and help the person heal. It has been effective, for example, in helping war veterans suffering from post-traumatic stress syndrome (PTSD). It helps the brain to associate a memory differently, so it becomes less disturbing.

MOTIVATIONAL THERAPIES

As the name implies, motivational therapies—the second-most common therapies used in treatment facilities—focus on encouraging a client to find the motivation or drive to overcome a substance addiction. Various approaches are used to encourage change, as opposed to teach a person in more explicit terms *how* to change. The emphasis is on ridding clients of self-doubt so they are confident in their ability to eliminate destructive behaviors.

- Motivational enhancement therapy (MET): Effective in treating alcohol, marijuana, and nicotine abuse, MET typically consists of between two and four treatment sessions. The treatment begins with the counselor encouraging motivational statements from the client and supporting this self-motivation. Counselor and client then talk about ways to handle "risky" situations—times and places where the client is vulnerable or likely to relapse. Follow-up sessions focus on ensuring change in behavior and motivation is maintained.
- Contingency management and motivational incentives: This is an award-system therapy of sorts, in which positive behavior is "reinforced" with concrete rewards—such as vouchers for retail goods and events like movie tickets in exchange for "clean" drug tests. This has been shown to be effective with alcohol, cocaine, methamphetamine, marijuana, nicotine, and prescription drug addictions.
- Community reinforcement: This is also a rewards-based system like the previously mentioned contingency management and motivational incentives approach and typically involves twenty-four therapy sessions with an emphasis on developing new hobbies, strengthening and improving relationships, and growing and deepening social support.

FAMILY COUNSELING AND THERAPIES

Substance abuse problems do not only affect the person with the actual problem. The consequences of living with and trying to manage a substance abuse problem spread far and wide into the lives of the people closest or most reliant on the person living with an addiction. This includes friends, family, and coworkers.

Families particularly suffer when a spouse, sibling, parent, or child has a substance abuse problem. The problems that result can be more easily navigated through family counseling sessions that improve understanding of the problem and communication techniques for addressing it and healing together.

- Family behavior therapy: This is therapy that aims to address how the substance abuse has impacted the family as a complete unit. Sessions usually involve several family members at the same time.

- Multisystemic family therapy: This is therapy focused on helping children and adolescents who have been affected by substance abuse to address and alleviate severe antisocial behavior that has resulted.
- Multidimensional family therapy: This therapy is geared toward teenagers who abuse substances. Its approaches help to encourage healthier behavior patterns and emphasizes effective problem-solving and decision-making skills.
- Brief strategic family therapy: Based on the idea that the behavior of each member of a family affects the family as a whole, this therapy addresses family interactions on issues that make teens particularly vulnerable to substance abuse, such as difficulties at school or with peer groups.

TWELVE-STEP FACILITATION THERAPY

For various types of substance abuse, including alcohol, cocaine, opioids, and methamphetamines, so-called twelve-step programs are likely the most familiar to the general public. The central commonality across twelve-step programs, regardless of the substance being abused, is that a person seeking treatment must accept that they have no control over the substance or the disease of addiction, that they must surrender to a higher power, and that they must attend group meetings to remain free of substance abuse. The best-known such program, Alcoholics Anonymous (AA), is the subject of a sidebar in this chapter.

ALTERNATIVE AND HOLISTIC THERAPIES

In addition to the more traditional therapies covered in this section, many substance abuse counselors are incorporating alternative or holistic therapy approaches in their work, and many people living with substance abuse issues are turning to these techniques to free themselves of their addictions.

NOTE: There is no hard evidence to support the effectiveness of these treatments as replacements for more traditional methods, but they have been shown to be effective as complementary treatments to these traditional approaches.

- Yoga, meditation, mindfulness: Practicing yoga, meditation, and mindfulness emphasizes breathing control, relaxation, and reducing stress and anxiety—all of which can be triggers for substance abuse.
- Acupuncture: A treatment that entails inserting small needles into a patient to promote healing, acupuncture is often offered in rehabilitation facilities as a complementary treatment and has been shown to be effective with cocaine addiction recovery in particular.
- Music and art therapy: Using music and art, clients are encouraged to experience, articulate, and engage with emotions, and such therapy can help increase and reinforce motivation.

Because every person combating a substance abuse problem is unique, from the roots of the addiction to the substance in question to the personality and circumstances of the person, there is no one-size-fits-all treatment for substance abuse. Therapies range from more traditional twelve-step programs to practicing mindfulness and meditation.
Goodboy Picture Company/E +/Getty Images

THE ROOTS AND RISE OF ALCOHOLICS ANONYMOUS (AA)

In 1935 in Akron, Ohio, a stockbroker (Bill W.) and a surgeon (Dr. Bob S.)—both alcoholics—met for the first time. Bill had gotten sober through the help of the Oxford Group, a Christian organization that was centered on the idea that the root of all problems was selfishness and fear, and the solution was to surrender oneself to God's plan. Through this influence, Bill had become sober, and through his influence and his belief that alcoholism was a malady of mind, emotions, and body, Dr. Bob also achieved sobriety. The men began working together with other alcoholics in the Akron area, and their approach quickly spread to New York (1935) and Cleveland, Ohio (1939).

The "Fellowship" they founded published a textbook in 1939, written by Bill and titled *Alcoholics Anonymous*. From there, AA developed quickly. Within a few months, there were five hundred members in Cleveland alone. The AA foundation opened an office in New York to distribute its book and respond to queries from an interested public. By 1941, the Fellowship spread across the United States and Canada, and by 1950 there were more than 100,000 reported recovered alcoholics worldwide.

AA is a twelve-step program. Reaching back to its Oxford Group roots, it requires first that members admit they are powerless over alcohol and need help from a "higher power" to mend. The twelve steps are:

1. We admitted we were powerless over alcohol—that our lives had become unmanageable.
2. Came to believe that a Power greater than ourselves could restore us to sanity.
3. Made a decision to turn our will and our lives over to the care of God as we understood Him.
4. Made a searching and fearless moral inventory of ourselves.
5. Admitted to God, to ourselves, and to another human being the exact nature of our wrongs.
6. Were entirely ready to have God remove all these defects of character.
7. Humbly asked Him to remove our shortcomings.
8. Made a list of all persons we had harmed, and became willing to make amends to them all.

9. Made direct amends to such people wherever possible, except when to do so would injure them or others.
10. Continued to take personal inventory and when we were wrong promptly admitted it.
11. Sought through prayer and meditation to improve our conscious contact with God, as we understood Him, praying only for knowledge of His will for us and the power to carry that out.
12. Having had a spiritual awakening as the result of these Steps, we tried to carry this message to alcoholics, and to practice these principles in all our affairs.

Although AA is the best known and somewhat go-to approach to alcoholics wanting to get sober (and it has inspired similar programs, such as Narcotics Anonymous), there are some researchers who question its science and effectiveness.[2] Although the program has undoubtedly helped many people worldwide for decades, for others the twelve-step approach did not work as well. This is why it's important that researchers and counselors continuously explore new approaches and methods when dealing with substance abuse problems because there is no one solution for everyone. Alternative approaches to AA will be discussed later in the book.

The Pros and Cons of Substance Abuse Counseling Careers

As with any career, one in substance abuse counseling carries with it upsides and downsides. But also true is that one person's pro is another person's con. If you consider yourself a strong interpersonal communicator and an attentive listener, you will likely thrive with in-person counseling sessions with groups or individuals. If you seek a reliable 9-to-5 life with a predictable schedule, you may struggle with the long hours and tendency for counselors to bring work home with them, if only mentally. There are lots of aspects to consider when choosing the right career for you.

TIP: Although it's one thing to read about the pros and cons of a particular career, the best way to really get a feel for what a typical day is like on the job and what the challenges and rewards are is to talk to someone who is already working in the profession or who has in the past.

Although there is a lot of variety within the substance abuse counseling field (as far as who you treat, where, and using what methods), there are some generalizations that can be made when it comes to what is most challenging about the job and what is most gratifying.

Here are some general pros:

- You will have the satisfaction that comes with a job that is challenging and educational and that is centered on helping people recover their health and livelihoods free from substance abuse.
- The job market is strong. Although it is unfortunate that substance abuse is a widespread problem, a reducing stigma surrounding seeking help and an increasingly diverse choice of therapy approaches are helping more people seek the help they need (and more insurance companies are helping cover the costs).
- You will have peers and colleagues who share your passion and from whom you can learn.
- It is a constantly evolving field with new trends and innovations and an endless opportunity for learning.
- There's a vast degree of variety in work environments, from prisons to schools to private practice to government-funded treatment centers, to name a few.

And here are some general cons:

- The working hours can be long and irregular. In some cases, counselors are on call twenty-four hours a day, seven days a week.
- The work is intensive. Listening carefully to clients every day all day can be mentally exhausting and even frustrating if a patient is not responding well or cooperating fully with therapy.
- It is a high-pressure field that requires an ability to manage stress well as well as to multitask.

- Substance abuse counseling can be emotionally draining. You may not be able to help everyone recover and that can be hard. Substance abuse counselors need to protect themselves against burnout.
- Starting your own practice, should you choose that path, can be a difficult and competitive process.

"To do well as a substance abuse counselor requires a solid understanding of science of human behavior, but that in itself is not sufficient. It is just as important that counselors be able to see the wisdom of clients' thoughts, feelings, and behaviors, particularly those the counselor does not necessarily agree with. Effective counselors need to listen for what is not being said and be able to collaborate with clients to solve problems creatively. Curiosity and compassion are indispensable."—Michael Ellery, substance abuse counselor

---

How Healthy Is the Job Market?

The job market for substance abuse counselors is quite strong—far stronger than other fields according to predications set by the Bureau of Labor Statistics (BLS). The BLS expects the job market to increase by 25 percent in the ten-year period between 2019 and 2029. Current estimates show the average annual income for a substance abuse counselor in the United States is $46,240 annually and $22.23 hourly.[3] A previous prediction made by the Department of Labor, predicted a 22 percent increase in the job market for substance abuse counseling between 2018 and 2028, during which time an additional 68,500 jobs were expected to become available.[4]

This is good news for the job market, but does it speak to a growing societal problem? The staggering number of people worldwide suffering from a substance abuse disorder was increased by the opioid epidemic, which reports now show has worsened due to the coronavirus disease pandemic and the psychological effects of lockdown.[5] In addition—and this news is more positive—changes in the criminal justice system in the United States have led to more

According to the World Drug Report as published by the United Nations in 2019, 35 million people globally are estimated to suffer from drug abuse disorders severe enough to require treatment, yet only one in seven sufferers receives the treatment they need to reach recovery.
LeszekCzerwonka/iStock/Getty Images

people who commit crimes being sent to drug and alcohol abuse treatment centers instead of jail as part of their sentence. Another reason for the increased demand for substance abuse counselors is the relative surge in recent years of military veterans seeking treatment, with one in ten veterans diagnosed with some form of substance abuse disorder.[6]

NOTE: The opioid epidemic refers to the growing number of deaths and hospitalizations from opioids, including prescriptions, illicit drugs, and analogues. In recent years, death rates from these drugs have ramped up to more than 40,000 a year, or 115 a day, across the United States, according to some sources.[7] These drugs include codeine, Demerol, heroin, methadone, morphine, oxycodone, and fentanyl.

WHAT IS A MEDIAN INCOME?

Throughout your job search, you might hear the term *median income* used. What does it mean? Some people believe it's the same thing as average income, but that's not correct. Although the median income and average income might sometimes be similar, they are calculated in different ways.

The true definition of median income is the income at which half of the workers earn more than that income and the other half of workers earn less. If this is complicated, think of it this way: Suppose there are five employees in a company, each with varying skills and experience. Here are their salaries:

- $42,500
- $48,250
- $51,600
- $63,120
- $86,325

What is the median income? In this case, the median income is $51,600 because of the five total positions listed, it is in the middle. Two salaries are higher than $51,600, and two are lower.

The average income is simply the total of all salaries, divided by the number of total jobs. In this case, the average income is $58,359.

Why does this matter? The median income is a more accurate way to measure the various incomes in a set because it's less likely to be influenced by extremely high or low numbers in the total group of salaries. For example, in our example of five incomes, the highest income ($86,325) is much higher than the other incomes, and therefore, it makes the average income ($58,359) well higher than most incomes in the group. Therefore, if you base your income expectations on the average, you'll likely be disappointed to eventually learn that most incomes are below it.

But if you look at median income, you'll always know that half the people are above it, and half are below it. That way, depending on your level of experience and training, you'll have a better estimate of where you'll end up on the salary spectrum.

Am I Right for a
Substance Abuse Counseling Career?

So, is substance abuse counseling the right career choice for you? This is a tough question to answer because really the answer can only come from you. But don't despair: There are plenty of resources both online and elsewhere that can help you find the answer by guiding you through the types of questions and considerations that will help you understand the requirements of a particular job and what characteristics and commitments are required to succeed in it. Examples of these are covered in more detail in chapter 2.

Thinking about what kind of career suits you the best can feel frustrating and intimidating, because it requires you to ask yourself important questions that only you can answer. There are, however, many sources online that can direct you to understand what characteristics a particular job, such as counseling, relies on the most to help you decide if it's a good fit.
GooGlobalStock/E +/Getty Images

For now, let's look at the general demands and responsibilities of a substance abuse counseling career—as were mentioned previously in the section on pros and cons—and suggest some questions that may help you discover whether such a profession is a good match for your personality, interests, and the general lifestyle you want to keep in the future.

Although there is not one "type" that matches the profile of a successful substance abuse counselor, there are some aspects of the job that you can anticipate and think about whether it sounds like something you would naturally enjoy or expect to struggle with.

NOTE: Of course, no job is going to match your personality or fit your every desire, especially when you are just starting out. There are, however, some aspects to a job that may be so unappealing or simply mismatched that you may decide to opt for something else, or equally you may be so drawn to a feature of a job that any downsides are not that important.

One way to see if you may be cut out for a career as a substance abuse counselor is to ask yourself the following questions:

- **Do I genuinely care about other people?**
  The central role of a counselor of any type, be it addiction, relationship, or what have you, is to help another person overcome a difficulty that is having a negative impact on their lives—to understand and resolve issues that are affecting their well-being. Although most people will say that yes, they care about others, that is not the same as dedicating your career to making other people's lives better.
- **Am I a trustworthy confidant? Am I able to keep secrets and preserve the confidentiality others entrust in me?**
  As a counselor, your success will depend on clients being able to freely and confidently open up to you and to share feelings and experiences they may never have openly discussed with another person. Other than in some cases where a confession relates to a crime, counseling sessions are expected to remain only between counselor and client. If you can't keep a secret, this is not the field for you.
- **Am I naturally inquisitive, and do I know how to ask the right questions to lead to deeper understanding of an issue?**
  A natural curiosity and excellent listening skills are paramount to an effective substance abuse counselor's success. A talent for digging deeply

enough to arrive at the root of an issue is needed to find the right approach to resolving a problem.

- **Am I tolerant and nonjudgmental?**
Substance abuse counselors have a responsibility to be tolerant and to be nonjudgmental in their practices.
- **Can I consistently deal with people in a professional, friendly way?**
Communication—naturally—is key to success in the substance abuse counseling field. Your interpersonal communication skills need to be exceptional when interacting with clients and their families to have effective and open discussions about the issues at hand and the approach to treatment being taken.
- **Do I have an overly excited attention to detail and an inability to leave any stone unturned?**
Do you give up easily or do you have the fortitude to keep probing, keep thinking, and keep searching for new answers and approaches? Not every client will respond straight away to treatment or counseling, and a successful counselor needs to be able to commit to a long-term relationship in some cases to help someone through their substance abuse problem.
- **At the same time, can I function under pressure?**
Counseling is not the kind of profession that enables you to shut down your computer at 5 p.m. and go home and think about something else until the next morning. Counselors are vulnerable to taking their work home with them and to being available at all hours. To avoid burnout, it is important to have strategies to deal with this kind of pressure as well as the emotional drain of thinking deeply about other people's struggles.

DOING THE WORK SHE WAS BORN TO DO

Michelle Hominick Anderson has been a registered social worker since 2008, receiving her bachelor's in social work in 2009 and master's in social work in 2015, both from the University of Manitoba. She has worked in a variety of practice settings including a nonprofit nongovernmental organization focusing on geriatric

Michelle Hominick Anderson.
Courtesy of Michelle Hominick Anderson.

mental health and addictions, a community hospital emergency department, inpatient and outpatient mental health, oncology clinic, nursing stations in several First Nations communities under contract with First Nations and Inuit Health Branch, and private practice, both as an associate and later as a managing partner and therapist. She currently co-owns Floating Bridge Therapy Services, a dialectical behavior therapy clinic in Winnipeg, where they specialize in working with people who live with borderline personality disorder. She is also a field instructor for students pursuing their master's in social work and delivers lectures on cognitive behavioral therapy, dialectical behavioral therapy, borderline personality disorder, and trauma-informed care.

How did you choose substance abuse counseling as a career?

I remember the day I found social work. I started university believing I was going to be an English teacher. During my first year, I took an Intro to Psychology class, and I was HOOKED! I switched tracks and started taking all the psychology classes I could, focusing mostly on behaviorism and perception. Then, when I was three years into my Honors BA in Psychology, I started feeling that something was missing from all of the courses I was taking. Where was the pursuit of social justice? Where was the heart? I searched on the University of Manitoba website, reviewing the information about a number of faculties, and then I found it; social work had everything that was important to me. I consider it a calling more than a career. If you ask my father, he will tell you I have been fighting for what is right since I could speak. I truly believe I was born to do this work. Over my time as a social worker, I have had the opportunity to work with many people struggling with substance use, and I have found it very rewarding albeit challenging work.

Can you describe your educational background and career path to date?

I did my bachelor's in social work (BSW) field placement at Jewish Child & Family Services where I learned about child and family service policies and procedures, therapy, and community social work. I was the first person to hold the Geriatric Mental Health & Addictions role in that agency. I worked there, learning everything I could from the more experienced social workers, for about four years. I applied for a job with Winnipeg Regional Health Authority at Grace Hospital, starting in the Emergency Department. That was the same year I started my master's in social work, and it took me three years to complete my degree. While I was on maternity leave with my youngest child, I did my master's in social work (MSW) Practicum at Victoria Hospital on their dialectical behavior therapy (DBT) team and with their inpatient mental health unit, facilitating groups and individual therapy. I think the thing that made me most prepared for the work I do now was finding a way to write every paper and do every assignment on some facet of cognitive behavioral therapy (CBT), wherever possible. The programs didn't provide an opportunity to specialize, so I made my own CBT program. There are many useful CBT-based interventions for treating addictions, including motivational interviewing and DBT.

I worked in various positions at Grace Hospital and got my MSW during my employment there, but when a change in government resulted in what I perceived to be unethical changes in the way the healthcare system functioned, particularly the mental health system, I knew it was time to leave. I became a traveling therapist with First Nations and Inuit Health Branch (FNIHB), going up to various First Nations communities and providing therapy and suicide risk assessments, and I also held an associate contract at a psychology clinic. My time working in Indigenous communities has really added to my understanding of working with people who live with addictions. When COVID hit, the psychology clinic owner chose to shut down, so another associate and I opened our own clinic. I think I always dreamed of opening my own clinic, but I certainly didn't think it would be this soon.

What is a typical day on the job for you?

COVID has resulted in work being anything but "typical." I am incredibly grateful to be in a profession that has been able to continue working virtually through the pandemic. Given it does not appear the COVID workday is going to shift back to pre-COVID anytime soon, I will describe what is typically happening for me now. I live with chronic pain, and it takes me a long time to get moving, so my workday starts at around 10 a.m. I will check emails, respond to anything urgent, check for cancellations, and look at who I will see in the day. I pull all the charts I will need and gather any resources that I anticipate using. I typically see five patients a day, all virtually. In between patients I do the case notes, graze in the kitchen, drink eighty-five cups of coffee, perhaps throw in some laundry, and play with the dogs. My clinic runs two groups per week, and one is in the evening, so that workday is usually ten hours long. We have our DBT team meeting once per week and I supervise my MSW student(s) once per week. And there is always some kind of paperwork to do with billing and outreach letters or creating forms. When I compare the pace, balance, and satisfaction of my current workday to the type of workday I had while I was working at the hospital, I honestly can't believe I did that for as long as I did. While I will remain forever grateful for everything I learned while I was at the hospital, I know I could never work in an environment like that again. Once we are able to see patients in the clinic, my day will include travel time as I live in the country, and probably significantly less laundry and dog-petting, though I do crave human interaction and look forward to seeing my coworkers daily.

When I am working in Indigenous communities at the nursing stations, we usually start our day with rounds. I receive referrals there and I hear about how the patients are struggling in various aspects. Then it was a lot of phone calling and outreach to try and get patients to come in to be seen. Being a mental health therapist with FNIHB means you are on call for twenty-four hours a day. I would often be called out in the middle of the night to help in cases of trauma, suicide attempts and/or ideation, or substance use issues. In Shamattawa, a lot of people struggle with addiction, and unfortunately, I had the experience of performing CPR and participating in Code Blue events. I witnessed death several times, and as a therapist, after the patient is pronounced dead, I had to switch gears to provide support to the family. I recall several instances when the nursing station would be packed with grieving family members, and I would make tea and walk around with cookies to hand out, offering my condolences. I have attempted to start addictions groups in every community I have attended, and generating interest and regular attendance is a real struggle.

What's the best or most satisfying part of your job?

The moments when the patient "gets it." When you are working with someone, trying to get them un-stuck, over the speed bump they're faced with on their life's journey, and something clicks for them, that feels like magic. Helping people understand how and why they have emotions, how the inability to regulate emotions creates urges to soothe with substances, and teaching the patients what the heck to do with emotions when they are there, other than use substances, is incredibly satisfying. It is such an honor to be trusted like this, to receive their stories, to hear about their darkest fears and secrets, and to observe their success as they conquer their goals. We are, each of us, the expert on our own life, and when a patient realizes they are perfectly capable of doing what they need to do in order to help themselves, the shift in their emotional state is palpable. I always tell my patients that my overall goal with them is to ultimately get fired, to which they always laugh, and then I explain that the most satisfying part of my job is working with someone until they no longer need my help, and they can achieve their goals and maintain their recovery without me.

What's the most challenging part or stressful part of your job?

All. The. PAPERWORK. Opening up your own clinic means you need to create a document for everything, a policy for everything, learn new things, be very organized, all while trying to do the actual work you want to do which is to provide therapy to patients. I suppose the good news is that, once you create a document, it is done, and you theoretically do not have to redo it for a while. I suppose I just didn't realize the sheer volume of forms and documents that would have to be created, but fortunately I am in charge of all of this, my managing partner and I are always able to find a synthesis when we have different ideas about what to do, and despite having many responsibilities and commitments, I feel more freedom now than in any other practice setting I have worked in.

In Indigenous communities, the most challenging part would have to be earning trust. Unfortunately, so many community members have experienced loss, trauma, and abuse, and it can be challenging to break through the walls they put up to protect themselves.

What has been the most surprising thing about your job as a substance abuse counselor?

This is a difficult question to answer. The more patients you work with, the less and less you are surprised by what they say. I would say the times over my career when I have been most surprised are when I witness my fellow social workers not acting in line with our social work values. I have seen a few cases where I observed unethical behavior from mental health therapists in Indigenous communities. It is also surprising when I see policy or practice that falls out of line with our social work code of ethics. I believe and respect our social work values and ethics to the depths of my soul, and I would never feel comfortable doing something or carrying out orders that violated those ethics. Ultimately, as social workers it is our responsibility to stand up and say something when policy or practice puts our patients at risk, but it is a hard lesson to learn when standing up is ineffective for change or, at worst, gets you into trouble. I think we have to learn to pick our battles, and I think that takes experience over time.

What kinds of qualities and personal characteristics do you consider advantageous to doing your job successfully?

I think having a great capacity for empathy is fundamentally important to our profession, and particularly in working with people who live with addictions. Being able to hear what the patient isn't saying and being able to provide critical feedback to them in a way that does not damage your relationship with them is essential. To own a clinic, you must be incredibly dedicated to providing effective treatment, and you have to be able to look at what you are currently doing and identify weak spots for improvement. Operating with an absence of ego, with constant vigilance about how your own vulnerabilities may be impacting on the way you are providing therapy, and how your blind spots may be clouding your clinical judgment, is very necessary. As therapists, and as humans, we are fallible and we will make mistakes, and it is crucial to be able to admit these mistakes to your patients and to yourself. I think what I have learned over the years is that I cannot fix anyone, and their recovery is outside the bounds of what I can control; people have to make their own mistakes and help themselves, so letting go of that desire for control is a skill unto itself. I think it is important to understand that addiction is a symptom of a greater problem, which is a failure to possess the adequate skills to regulate emotions effectively, in the context of an environment that reinforces ineffective behavior, and that does not provide adequate supports. To work in Indigenous communities, you have to understand that they are the experts on how their community will best function, and you cannot implement changes or programming without the approval and advice of Chief and Council. Be humble, listen to the Elders, and assume they know better than you do about what they need in order for their community to thrive.

How do you combat burnout?

I think removing myself from a system I no longer believed in was fundamental to addressing my burnout. Nothing burns social workers out more than seeing people in need and feeling totally powerless to help them, whether that powerlessness be due to oppressive policies and procedures of the agency, lack of effective supervision to help you improve your practice, lack of training to provide effective interventions, or anything in between. Goodness of fit between a social worker and the values of the agency in which they work is a good first step to avoiding burnout. Boundaries are essential in this work, and understanding how much of yourself to give to your practice, where your limits are, and learning to respect them, is critically important. Personally, I try to be organized so I know what I need to do, and when I need to do it, so I don't feel overwhelmed by things piling up. I engage in as much self-care as possible, and when I am tired or in pain, I take a break. I schedule my patients around necessary personal appointments, and I avoid the urge to feel guilty when I simply cannot do everything and see everyone I want to see. While I was at Jewish Child & Family Services, I learned a Yiddish expression which roughly translates to: If I am not for myself, who will be for me? It is along the lines of the idea that we cannot pour from an empty cup, that if we don't take care of ourselves, we cannot effectively help anyone else, and we are the only person who can know when we need self-care. I have carried this idea with me through my whole career to date, and it has yet to fail me.

How do you see your career or the substance abuse field evolving in the future?

As far as the future of my career is concerned, I have many dreams and aspirations for my clinic, and I consider myself very fortunate that my work partner has the same kinds of big ideas. I don't ever see myself moving away from self-employment absolutely, though I have thought of pursuing a PhD in the future should I decide to move out of practice and into teaching at the university. After all, I started university all those years ago hoping to be a teacher, and I very much enjoy the teaching aspects of my work. For now, I am focusing on growing my clinic and trying to provide the most effective service possible.

As far as the future of the social work field and addictions counseling is concerned, I have noticed less and less clinical emphasis in the MSW programs I have seen, and this makes me very uneasy. Clinical social work is an important part of the mental health system, and I worry that putting less emphasis on clinical practice in our educational programs will mean insurance companies and agencies will start to become reluctant to cover our services, and social workers will be less competitive for fewer clinical jobs. As far as I am concerned, a clinical social worker has the potential to be the most effective mental health clinician available due to our focus on the micro to macro, coupled with our social work ethics, and contributed to by what previously was quite effective clinical training—I truly believe we are perhaps the best-suited clinicians to help people who struggle with addictions in the most effective ways. I am hopeful that educational institutions will offer more clinical training for their MSW students in the future, and even specifically for those who want to work with people who struggle with addictions, and I am happy to do what I can to improve this situation by offering clinical MSW placements at my clinic.

Summary

This chapter covered a lot of ground as far as looking more closely as the various types of therapy approaches, clients, and work environments available within the substance abuse counselor field. The career outlook for the substance abuse counselor is quite strong, with an above-average growth prediction (compared with other careers) of 25 percent over the next ten years.

Here are some ideas to take away with you as you move on to the next chapter:

- Substance abuse counseling is an exciting and changing field, in which new research into innovative and complementary treatments is conducted continuously, while older, more traditional methods are refined.
- No two days are alike for a substance abuse counselor, which makes it an exciting field in which you are continuously challenged and constantly learning.
- As a substance abuse counselor, you can choose from many different work environments, from schools to prisons, from government-funded treatment centers to private practices.
- Substance abuse counselors work with a variety of clients from all backgrounds, age groups, socioeconomic and geographic circumstances, and career and educational levels. Anyone can have a substance abuse problem, and counselors can choose to practice for a specific group if they choose.
- As a profession, substance abuse counseling has a healthy outlook, with a high percentage of career growth over the next ten years.

Given all you now know about the job of a substance abuse counselor, you may still be questioning whether such a career is right for you. This chapter provided some questions that can help you visualize yourself in real-world situations you can expect to face on the job to help you guide your decision process.

Assuming you are now more enthusiastic than ever about pursuing a career in substance abuse counseling, in the next chapter we will look more closely at how you can refine your choice to a more specific job. It offers tips and advice and how to find the role and work environment that will be most satisfying to you and what steps you can start taking—immediately!—toward reaching your future career goals.

2

Forming a Career Plan

*N*o pressure, but choosing a career is one of the important decisions you will make in your life. There are simply so many options available, and it is easy to feel overwhelmed. Particularly if you have many passions and interests, it can be hard to narrow your options down. That you are reading this book means you have decided to investigate a career in the field of substance abuse counseling, which means you have already discovered a passion for helping people, working to resolve societal issues, encouraging health and well-being, effective communication, and continuous learning.

But even within the counseling field, there are many choices, including what role you want to pursue, in what environment you desire to work, and what type of work schedule best fits your lifestyle. It's a lot to think about, but fortunately it's also exciting to consider your options, particularly because it's a decision that is primarily based on aspects of you (your interests, natural gifts, curiosities) that you know more about than anyone else.

TIP: This may all sound dramatic and even scary. Keep in mind as you consider your career options that it is common to change your mind or shift gears at any stage in your career. Be thoughtful about your decisions, but don't put too much pressure on yourself. It's not a case of only getting one chance to decide.

A career in counseling—including substance abuse counseling—is in some ways a specific choice of career, but it also offers a lot of choice and variety as far as who your clients are, what therapies or treatments you will apply, in what environment you will work, and how you can contribute to the field through research or working directly with clients and their families.

Before you can plan the path to a successful career in the industry—such as by committing to a college program—it's helpful to develop an understanding of what role you want to have and in what environment you wish to work. Do you want to work in an established treatment center or publicly funded facility, or do you prefer the more entrepreneurial feel of a private practice? Do you want to work specifically with young people? Or maybe you want to focus on researching new approaches to rehabilitation. Are you willing to relocate? Work long hours and weekends? These are all things to consider.

It's also important to think about how much education would you like to pursue? Depending on your ultimate career goal, the steps to getting there differ. Jobs in counseling will typically require bachelor's degree or higher, and specific certifications may be required before you can practice. You can choose to study anything that relates to counseling, behavioral science, psychology, or mental health science. . . . the choices are many, and we will look at them a bit in this chapter and even more specifically, as well as discussing particular schools that offer programs of interest.

Deciding on a career means asking yourself big questions, but there are several tools and assessment tests that can help you determine what your personal strengths and aptitudes are and with which career fields and environments they best align. These tools guide you to think about important factors in choosing a career path, such as how you respond to pressure and how effectively—and how much you enjoy—working and communicating with people. These will be discussed in this chapter as well.

YOUR PASSIONS, ABILITIES, AND INTERESTS: IN JOB FORM!

Think about how you've done at school and how things have worked out at any temporary or part-time jobs you've had so far. What are you really good at, in your opinion? And what have other people told you you're good at? What are you not good at right now, but you would like to become better at? What are you not good at, and you're okay with not getting better at?

Now forget about work for a minute. In fact, forget about needing to ever have a job again. You won the lottery—congratulations. Now answer these questions: What are your favorite three ways of spending your time? For each one of those things, can you describe why you think you in particular are attracted to it? If you could get up tomorrow and do anything you wanted all day long, what would it be? These questions can be fun, but they can also lead you to your true passions. The next step is to find the job that sparks your passions.

This chapter explores the educational requirements for various careers within the counseling field, as well as options for where to go for help when planning your path to the career you want. It offers advice on how to begin preparing for your career path at any age or stage in your education, including in high school.

Planning the Plan

So where to begin? Before taking the leap and applying to or committing in your mind to a particular college or program, there are other considerations and steps you can take to map out your plan for pursuing your career. Preparing your career plan begins with developing a clear understanding of what your actual career goal is.

Planning your career path means asking yourself questions that will help shape a clearer picture of what your long-term career goals are and what steps to take to achieve them. When considering these questions, it's important to prioritize your answers—when listing your skills, for example, put them in order of strongest to weakest. When considering questions relating to how you want to balance your career with the rest of your nonwork life, such as family and hobbies, really think about what your top priorities are and in what order.

The following are questions that are helpful to think about deeply when planning a career path.

- Think about your interests outside of the work context. How do you like to spend your free time? What inspires you? What kind of people do you like to surround yourself with, and how do you best learn? What do you really love doing? (Hint: If you find you are impatient when others discuss their personal problems, counseling may not be for you!)

- Brainstorm a list of the various career choices within the counseling/ helping others arena that you are interested in pursuing (think about whether you are interested in science as it relates to mental health and addiction, in healing others, in tackling societal issues, in interpersonal communication). Organize the list in order of which careers you find most appealing, and then list what it is about each that attracts you. This can be anything from work environment to geographical location to the degree in which you would work with other people in a particular role.
- Research information on each job on your career choices list. You can find job descriptions, salary indications, career outlook, salary, and educational requirements information online, for example. Some of this information was provided in chapter 1.
- Consider your personality traits. This is important to finding which jobs "fit" you and which almost certainly do not. How do you respond to stress and pressure? Do you consider yourself a strong communicator? Do you work well in teams or prefer to work independently? Do you consider yourself creative? How do you respond to criticism? Are you curious and thorough? All of these are important to keep in mind to ensure you choose a career path that makes you happy and in which you can thrive.
- Although a career choice is obviously a huge factor in your future, it's important to consider what other factors feature in your vision of your ideal life. Think about how your career will fit in with the rest of your life, including whether you want to live in a big city or small town, how much flexibility you want in your schedule, how much autonomy you want in your work, and what your ultimate career goal is.
- The job of a substance abuse counselor is a sensitive one that carries some high stakes: helping a person modify their behaviors that are sabotaging to their health, well-being, and relationships. Whether you work in an in-patient rehabilitation center or private practice, for example, your role will be to guide clients through their recovery journey, which will likely entail relapses and crises along the way. Some of the most fulfilling and meaningful work can also be the most taxing, emotionally and physically, demanding long and irregular hours. Because succeeding in the counseling field requires so much commitment, it's important to

think about how willing you are to put in long hours and perform what can be demanding work—without burning out.

- Many job opportunities that offer experience to newcomers and recent graduates can come with relatively low salaries. What are your pay expectations, now and in the future?

Posing these questions to yourself and thinking about them deeply and answering them honestly will help make your career goals clearer and guide you in knowing which steps you will need to take to get there.

Although all jobs can be stressful at times, especially when one is deeply committed to doing their job well, the role of a substance abuse counselor can be exceptionally draining because of its sensitive and personal nature and the possibility of working long or irregular hours. It's important to develop strategies for combating burnout.
fanjianhua/Moment/Getty Images

Where to Go for Help

Again, the process of deciding on and planning a career path is daunting. In many ways, the range of choices of careers available today is a wonderful thing.

It allows us to refine our career goals and customize them to our own lives and personalities. In other ways, though, too much choice can be extremely daunting and require a lot of soul-searching to navigate clearly.

Answering questions about your habits, characteristics, interests, and personality can be challenging. Identifying and prioritizing all of your ambitions, interests, and passions can be overwhelming and complicated. It's not always easy to see yourself objectively or see a way to achieve what matters most to you, but there are several resources and approaches to help guide you in drawing conclusions about these important questions.

- Take a career assessment test to help you answer questions about what career best suits you. There are several available online.
- Consult with a career or personal coach to help you refine your understanding of your goals and how to pursue them.
- Talk with professionals working in the job you are considering and ask them what they enjoy about their work, what they find the most challenging, and what path they followed to get there.
- Educate yourself as much as possible about the field: what are the latest research breakthroughs or trends in substance abuse therapies? What are the latest statistics about substance abuse problems in the United States and beyond? Stay current as much as possible with topics relating to the career you wish to pursue.
- Although it may not be possible to "job shadow"—accompany someone during their workday to witness firsthand what a typical day on the job is like—a counselor for privacy reasons, you can likely arrange to visit a treatment center or hospital to get a sense of the environment.

ONLINE RESOURCES TO HELP YOU PLAN YOUR PATH

The Internet is an excellent source of advice and assessment tools that can help you find and figure out how to pursue your career path. Some of these tools focus on an individual's personality and aptitude, and others can help you identify and improve your skills to prepare for your career.

In addition to the following sites, you can use the Internet to find a career or life coach near you—many offer their services online as well. Job sites such as LinkedIn are a good place to search for people working in a profession you'd like to learn more about or to explore the types of jobs available as a substance abuse counselor.

- At educations.com, you will find a career test designed to help you find the job of your dreams. Visit https://www.educations.com/career-test to take the test.
- The *Princeton Review* has created a career quiz that focuses on personal interests: https://www.princetonreview.com/quiz/career-quiz.
- To specifically discover whether you should become a substance abuse counselor, check out OwlGuru.com, which offers a one-minute online quiz: https://www.owlguru.com/career/substance-abuse-and-behavioral-disor der-counselors/quiz/.
- The Bureau of Labor Statistics provides information, including quizzes and videos, to help students up to grade 12 explore various career paths. The site also provides general information on career prospects and salaries. Visit BLS.gov to find these resources.

NOTE: Young adults with disabilities can face additional challenges when planning a career path. Disabilities, Opportunities, Internetworking, and Technology (DO-IT) is an organization dedicated to promoting career and education inclusion for everyone. Its website contains a wealth of information and tools to help all young people plan a career path, including self-assessment tests and career exploration questionnaires: https://www.washington.edu/doit/preparing-career-online-tutorial.

Making High School Count

Once you have narrowed down your interests and have a fairly strong idea what type of career you want to pursue, you naturally want to start putting your career path plan into motion as quickly as you can. If you are a high school student, you may feel there isn't much you can do toward achieving your career goals—other than, of course, earning good grades and graduating. But there are actually many ways you can make your high school years count toward your career in substance abuse counseling before you have earned your high school diploma. This section will cover how you can use this period of your education and life to better prepare you for your career goal and to ensure you keep your passion alive while improving your skill set.

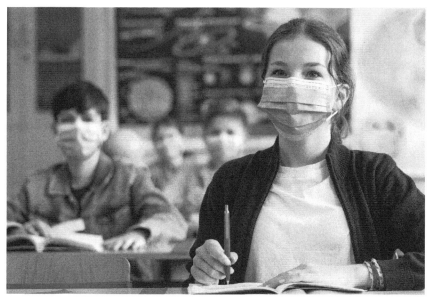

Even while still in high school, there are many ways you can begin working toward your career goal. Classes in another language, in writing, in interpersonal communication, and health can all help you prepare for a career as a substance abuse counselor.
zusek/E +/Getty Images

COURSES TO TAKE IN HIGH SCHOOL

Depending on your high school and what courses you have access to, there are many subjects that will help you prepare for a career in substance abuse counseling. Beyond doing your own research into different areas of counseling and different work environments and the types of clients you may serve in the future, you can take advantage of any college prep courses your school offers, particularly in areas relating to psychology or sociology but also in subjects such as public speaking or literature to help you strengthen your communication skills.

TIP: Taking advanced placement (AP) courses while in high school (assuming you pass the AP exam at the end of the course) may enable you to earn college credit early and skip taking elementary or introductory courses in the subject (for example, psychology) when you get to college.

Here are some courses, college prep or standard level, that you should pursue while in high school. Some of them may seem unrelated initially, but they will all help you prepare yourself and develop key skills.

- Language arts. Communication is a key part of working as a counselor of any kind because it is a job that will demand you be an effective communicator in writing and verbally.
- Math. Research requires an understanding of math, how to interpret statistics, and percentages and to put them into terms you, your colleagues, a client, and a client's family will understand.
- Interpersonal communication/public speaking. These courses will be an asset in any profession but especially in counseling. Encouraging people to open up to you about their personal struggles requires them to feel comfortable doing so, which will depend on your interpersonal communication skills.
- A second language. To expand your clientele and be able to reach more people in need of substance abuse counseling, learning a second language will be a great asset.
- Business and economics. If you imagine yourself running a private practice, you will need to have business and accounting skills as well as those required to be a qualified counselor.

GAINING WORK EXPERIENCE

The best way to learn anything is to do it. When it comes to preparing for a career in substance abuse counseling or any type of counseling, you can consider becoming a peer counselor or volunteering at a mental health facility in your community.

Volunteering in this way will provide you valuable training in areas such as recognizing symptoms of substance abuse or mental health disorders and help you improve the qualities of an effective counselor, such as patience, compassion, and good listening and communication skills.

Find out if your school offers any opportunities for volunteering, such as a peer-counseling group. You can also contact local health clinics and organizations to seek out volunteer opportunities there.

CAN HYPNOSIS HELP AN ADDICT TO QUIT?

Although the word *hypnosis* tends to conjure an image of a stage performer waving a watch back and forth and making their subject sleepy, there is some evidence that hypnosis, when properly performed, can help aid a person in ceasing damaging habits, such as drinking and other forms of substance abuse. There has not been much scientific research into its efficacy, but there is some support for the idea that hypnosis—particularly when combined with more traditional counseling—can bring about positive behavioral change in some people. This is because hypnosis helps bring a person to a relaxed state, which causes them to be more receptive to suggestion.

A 2018 study[1] investigated the efficacy of hypnotherapy for treating alcohol abuse. For the study, thirty-one adults in an inpatient program for alcohol use disorder were attending group counseling and other activities as part of treatment, as well as one hour of individual therapy each week. During these private sessions, half of the group received hypnotherapy in place of the usual treatment.

The hypnotherapy involved asking the participants to visualize themselves resisting urges to drink alcohol applying various strategies, including remaining calm when stressful situations present triggers to drink, turning down a drink at an event, or not entering a store where alcohol is sold.

When following up on the study a year later, researchers found evidence to suggest the following:

- All participants who responded to the follow-up reported a significant decrease in alcohol use.
- Participants in the hypnotherapy group reported slightly less emotional distress.
- Nine participants in the hypnotherapy group reported complete abstinence, as opposed to seven participants in the motivational interview group.

So although more research needs to be done to support hypnotherapy as an effective part of a substance abuse treatment, it is certainly being considered by professionals and those seeking help with a substance abuse problem.

Educational Requirements

You will have to pursue education beyond high school to become a substance abuse counselor. The level of education you pursue is up to you; but keep in mind the higher a degree you earn, the better your chances are at securing employment and earning a higher salary.

Whatever type of job you want to pursue in substance abuse counseling, you should expect to have to earn at minimum a two-year associate degree to introduce you to the career and help you decide if you want to go further and earn a four-year bachelor's degree, which is recommended for substance abuse counseling careers. In other cases, a master's or even a doctorate is recommended. In addition, there are certificate programs you can earn at your community college or online to continue or broaden your education throughout your career.

HOW TO PREPARE FOR RUNNING YOUR PRIVATE PRACTICE

Although this chapter has already provided advice on the types of courses you should consider following in high school or higher education to help prepare you for success as a substance abuse counselor, if you have the ambition to run your own private practice, you will gain from even more business-related courses.

Running a business is its own challenge, on top of that of becoming a qualified substance abuse counselor. Mastering certain business skills is absolutely crucial to succeeding in running your own practice, from doing your own accounting to getting the word out to attract clients. Careers in Psychology offers the following advice regarding courses to take that will prepare you for the challenge of operating your own practice.[2]

1. **Accounting:** Take a lower-division accounting course. You will be responsible for managing the money for your business, and therefore, you will need to understand basic accounting concepts.

2. **Advertising:** Seek out courses that deal with the topic of advertising and promotion. If your campus does not offer any, look into online classes that would be convenient and time-efficient. Consider it a hobby instead of another class. Topics that will be helpful are ones that deal with promotional design, cost-effective advertising techniques, and anything else that will help your business become prominent in the public eye.

3. **Social Media Marketing:** Today's professional doesn't just rely on word of mouth, business cards, and a nicely painted sign to increase the traffic flow of their business. Savvy counselors have mastered the world of Twitter, LinkedIn, Google+, Facebook, etc. You may already have these skills under your belt, so begin to think in terms of how to effectively integrate them into the realm of a private counseling practice. Begin to look at counselors who are involved in marketing themselves through social media channels, and notice what you like and what changes you would make. Have fun with this; your imagination is your friend.

4. **Business Plan:** Anyone planning on success has some concept of what it means to devise a business plan. Basically, this is a well-researched, well-thought-out document that analyzes costs and projected income. This will be something you will need if you intend to seek out a loan from a bank or investor. If your college has a business major, go to the department offices and inquire as to the classes that might be appropriate for your endeavors. If this is not available or practical, begin to read online about what a business plan is and how to come up with one. Even if you do not plan on securing financial backing, a wise business owner always has a plan.

5. **Minor in Business:** If you are convinced you will want to go into private practice, you might consider choosing business as your minor. It may sound like something you really do not want to do. However, if you go into private practice it *will* be a fact that you *will* be doing business on a daily basis.

6. **Seminars on Small Business:** During your quarter or semester breaks, consider attending a small business seminar. It will be a fast and easy way to get some basics under your belt; it will also give you a heads up on what might lie ahead.

7. **Web Design Course:** Depending on finances, you may end up having to design a simple website for your practice. But even if you plan on hiring someone else to do it, knowing what you're paying for is always smart business. Find out what attracts the eye and what doesn't. Discover what appeals to different age groups and target your clientele.

"We are, each of us, the expert on our own life, and when a patient realizes they are perfectly capable of doing what they need to do in order to help themselves, the shift in their emotional state is palpable. I always tell my patients that my overall goal with them is to ultimately get fired, to which they always laugh, and then I explain that the most satisfying part of my job is working with someone until they no longer need my help, and they can achieve their goals and maintain their recovery without me."—Michelle Hominick Anderson, registered social worker and addiction counselor

WHY CHOOSE AN ASSOCIATE DEGREE?

A two-year degree—called an associate degree—is sufficient to give you a knowledge base to begin your career and can form as a basis should you decide to pursue a four-year degree later. If you are prepared to put in the financial and time commitment to earn an associate degree and are sure of the career goal you have set for yourself, consider earning a bachelor's instead. With so much competition out there, the more of an edge you can give yourself, the better your chances will be.

WHY CHOOSE A BACHELOR'S DEGREE?

A bachelor's degree—which usually takes four years to maintain—is a requirement in most cases for a career in substance abuse counseling. And in general, the higher education you pursue, the better your odds are to advance in your career, which means more opportunity and, often, more compensation.

The difference between an associate and a bachelor's degree is of course the amount of time each takes to complete. To earn a bachelor's degree, a candidate must complete forty college credits, compared with twenty for an associate degree. This translates to more courses completed and a deeper exploration of degree content, even though similar content is covered in both.

> NOTE: Even when not required, a master's degree can help advance your career, give you an edge over the competition in the field, and give you more specific knowledge relating to your work in substance abuse counseling.

WHY CHOOSE A MASTER'S DEGREE?

A master's degree is an advanced degree that usually takes two years to complete. A master's will offer you a chance to become more specialized and to build on the education and knowledge you gained while earning your bachelor's. A master's can be done directly after your bachelor's, although many people choose to work for a while in between to discover what type of master's degree is most relevant to their careers and interests. Many people also earn their master's degree while working full- or part-time.

> NOTE: In some instances, a doctorate will be required, depending on your career goals. If you have the desire to teach or perform research at the university level you will be required to hold a doctorate in a relevant subject.

"I OFTEN SUSPECT I HAVE THE BEST JOB IN THE WORLD"

Dr. Michael Ellery completed an honors bachelor's degree at the University of Winnipeg and a PhD in clinical psychology at Dalhousie University. He has worked as an addiction therapist at the Centre for Addiction and Mental Health in Toronto and as the clinical specialist for the Addictions Foundation of Manitoba in Winnipeg. He directed the Mental Health and Addiction Laboratory at the University of Manitoba while he was an assistant professor in their clinical psychology training program for six years. He still enjoys teaching and training addiction researchers

Michael Ellery.
Courtesy of Michael Ellery.

and therapists, now that he works as a licensed clinical psychologist in private practice. He lives with his partner and their daughter in Winnipeg, Manitoba, Canada.

How did you choose substance abuse counseling as a career?

Substance use problems touch the lives of so many people, both directly and indirectly. I probably came by my interest in substance use problems the way most of us do. Seeing how substance use problems affected the people in my life made me want to learn more about how I could help.

Can you describe your educational background and career path to date?

I am a clinical psychologist. In many places, being a licensed psychologist means you need a PhD or a PsyD degree. I have a PhD in clinical psychology. Depending on where you live, substance abuse counseling may or may not be a regulated health profession, meaning you may not need a license to practice.

To get hired as a substance abuse counselor, it used to be that a high school diploma and some lived experience as a person who is abstinent from drugs and alcohol were sufficient. Today, a person typically needs a bachelor's degree. In places where substance abuse counseling is not regulated, employers may still prefer candidates who are members of national accreditation bodies.

My path is not typical of people who want to be substance use counselors. I completed a four-year honors undergraduate degree program in psychology, and then a five-year PhD program in clinical psychology. During that time, I volunteered with organizations that help people with substance use problems. While finishing up my PhD, I worked in a hospital as an addiction therapist. Afterward, I worked as a professor in a clinical psychology training program for several years, where I trained psychologists to use scientifically supported therapies for problems with mental health and substance use. I was also the director of a research laboratory that studied mental health and addictive behaviors, and I taught both in the clinic and in the classroom. I left the academic job and briefly worked as a clinical specialist in a substance use treatment agency in the public health system before going into private practice full time. Most substance use counselors will not need as much education to work in the field.

What is a typical day on the job for you?

As a psychologist in private practice, much of my day is spent seeing clients for assessment and therapy. Other parts of my day include responding to requests for service or information, and handling scheduling and billing. At various points in my career, such as when working in the public health sector, my days included meetings with colleagues and supervisors to discuss client care, attending teachings and training, developing and delivering addiction and mental health information to colleagues and the public. The least fun part for many of us is keeping up with all of the health-related documentation, like clinical notes and reports, that comes with providing effective services to clients. The days of a substance use counselor would look pretty similar.

What's the best or most satisfying part of your job?

Seeing peoples' lives change as a result of all of their hard work is very satisfying. It is such a privilege to be part of their healing process. It is inspiring and indescribably moving to witness their courage and resourcefulness. I often suspect I have the best job in the world.

What's the most challenging part or stressful part of your job?

Substance use problems are complex, chronic, and prone to relapse. Health care systems are chronically under-resourced when it comes to the care of people who need help with mental health or substance use. Counseling can fail, even when it is done perfectly. And even when counseling does not fail, progress can be imperceptibly slow and frustrating for both clients and counselors. It is also painful when clients die, whether directly or indirectly as a result of their substance use.

What has been the most surprising thing about your job as a substance abuse counselor?

Maybe the most surprising thing was how much time a substance use counselor has to spend on administrative tasks.

What kinds of qualities and personal characteristics do you consider advantageous to doing your job successfully?

To do well as a substance abuse counselor requires a solid understanding of the science of human behavior, but that in itself is not sufficient. It is just as important that counselors be able to see the wisdom of clients' thoughts, feelings, and behaviors, particularly those the counselor does not necessarily agree with. Effective counselors need to listen for what is not being said and be able to collaborate with clients to solve problems creatively. Curiosity and compassion are indispensable.

How do you combat burnout?

Self-care is essential. Like every job, there is such a demand for service that the temptation can be strong to skip a meal, or a workout, in favor of working longer hours to help people. Substance use counselors need to be careful to follow the same advice we would give our clients to avoid burnout: balance yourdiet, exercise regularly, observe good sleep hygiene, develop your leisure activities, stay connected with others. A concern more unique to avoiding burnout as a substance use counselor is making sure you get enough training and supervision. Clients with substance use concerns can often have complex clinical needs. Consulting regularly with peers and supervisors is so important to ensure the needs of both counselors and clients are being met.

How do you see your career or the substance abuse field evolving in the future?

In some ways, the future seems to be now! Due to higher levels of stress and lower levels of stigma, requests for service are increasing. More services will be delivered via telecounseling, including by phone or online. Online assessments and therapies could soon be more regularly conducted by artificial intelligence. That said, given the interpersonal nature of the work, I suspect there will always be demand for in-person counseling, with a human being.

Summary

This chapter covered a lot of ground in terms of how to break down the challenge of not only discovering whether a career in substance abuse counseling is right for you and in what environment, capacity, and work culture you want to work but also how best to prepare yourself for achieving your career goal.

In this chapter, you learned about some of the specific training and educational options, requirements, and expectations that will put you, no matter what your current education level or age, at a strong advantage in a competitive field.

Use this chapter as a guideline for how to best discover what type of career will be the right fit for you and consider what steps you can already be taking to get there. Some tips to leave you with:

- Take time to carefully consider what kind of work environment you see yourself working in and what kind of schedule, interaction with colleagues, work culture, and responsibilities you want to have.
- Pay attention to current research and therapies to stay abreast of trends and important statistics in the field of substance abuse counseling.
- Talk with a professional to get a feeling for what hours they keep, what challenges they face, and what the overall job entails. Find out what education or training they completed before launching their career.
- Investigate various colleges and certification options so you can better prepare yourself for the next step in your career path. (More of this in chapter 3.)
- Don't feel you have to wait until you graduate from high school to begin taking steps to accomplish your career goals.
- Keep work-life balance in mind. The career you choose will be one of many adult decisions you make, and ensuring that you keep all of your priorities—family, location, work schedule—in mind will help you choose the right career for you, which will make you a happier person.

3

Pursuing the Educational Path

Making decisions about your educational path can be just as daunting as choosing a career. It is a decision that not only demands understanding what kind of education or training is required for the career you want but also what kind of school or college you want to attend. There is a lot to consider no matter what area of study you want to pursue and depending on the type of job you want to have within the field of substance abuse counseling.

Now that you've gotten an overview of the different degree options that can prepare you for your future career as a substance abuse counselor, this chapter will dig more deeply into how to best choose the right type of study plan for you. Even if you are years away from earning your high school diploma or equivalent, it's never too soon to start weighing your options, thinking about the application process, and of course, taking time to really consider what kind of educational track and environment will suit you best.

Not everyone wants to take time to go to college or pursue additional academic-based training, and for many careers, it is not required, even if recommended. However, a career in substance abuse counseling will require some level of higher education after you earn your high school degree or equivalent. It is not a field you can enter without earning certain qualifications.

So, if you are interested in and prepared to follow the educational path—from earning a certificate in substance abuse counseling to pursuing a four-year university degree or higher—this chapter will help you navigate the process of deciding on the type of institution you would most thrive in, determining what type of degree you want to earn, and looking into costs and how to find help in meeting them.

The chapter will also give you advice on the application process, how to prepare for any entrance exams such as the SAT or ACT that you may need to take, and how to communicate your passion, ambition, and personal experience in a personal statement. When you've completed this chapter, you should have a good sense of what kind of education beyond high school is right for you and how to ensure you have the best chance of being accepted at the institution of your choice.

NOTE: At the time of writing, the United States and beyond are experiencing a pandemic that has caused some of the traditional approaches to teaching and learning to change—hopefully just temporarily. This chapter is offering advice that assumes you will be applying to and attending educational institutions in person, which will hopefully be the case. Even if, for now, you are learning or virtually doing campus visits, the advice offered here is still relevant, although the way you engage with institutions, faculty members, or other students is a bit unorthodox for the time being.

Finding a Program or School That Fits Your Personality

Before we get into the details of good schools that offer degrees in subjects related to substance abuse counseling, it's a good idea for you to take some time to consider what "type" of school will be best for you. Just as with your future work environment, understanding how you best learn, what type of atmosphere best fits your personality, and how and where you are most likely to succeed will play a major part in how happy you will be with your choice. This section will provide some thinking points to help you refine what kind of school or program is the best fit for you.

CONSIDERING A GAP YEAR

Taking a year off between high school and college, often called a "gap year," is normal, perfectly acceptable, and almost required in many countries around the world, and it is becoming increasingly acceptable in the United States as well. Particularly if you want to pursue a career as a counselor, having exposure to the world outside of the classroom will help you gain perspective and experience that you can immediately apply to your future work. It can help you become more empathic, less judgmental, and a more open thinker. Because the cost of college has gone up dramatically, it literally pays for you to know going in what you want to study, and a gap year—well spent—can do lots to help you answer that question. It can also give you an opportunity to explore different places and people to help you find a deeper sense of what you'd like to study when your gap year has ended.

Some great ways to spend your gap year include joining the Peace Corps or other organizations that offer opportunities for work experience. A gap year can help you see things from a new perspective. Consider enrolling in a mountaineering program or other gap year–styled program, backpacking across Europe or other countries on the cheap (be safe and bring a friend), find a volunteer organization that furthers a cause you believe in or that complements your career aspirations, join a Road Scholar program (see www.roadscholar.org), teach English in another country (see https://www.gooverseas.com/blog/best-countries-for-seniors-to-teach-english-abroad for more information), or work and earn money for college!

Many students will find that they get much more out of college when they have a year to mature and to experience the real world. The American Gap Year Association reports from their alumni surveys that students who take gap years show improved civic engagement, improved college graduation rates, and improved GPAs in college.

See their website at https://gapyearassociation.org/ for lots of advice and resources if you're considering a potentially life-altering experience.

If nothing else, answering questions like the following ones can help you narrow your search and focus on a smaller sampling of choices. Write your answers down to these questions somewhere where you can refer to them often, such as in your notes app on your phone:

- *Size*: Does the size of the school matter to you? Colleges and universities range from sizes of 500 or fewer students to 25,000 students. If you are considering college or university, think about what size of class you would like, and what the right instructor-to-student ratio is for you.
- *Community location:* Would you prefer to be in a rural area, a small town, a suburban area, or a large city? How important is the location of the school in the larger world to you? Is the flexibility of an online degree or certification program attractive to you, or do you prefer more on-site, hands-on instruction?

- *Length of study:* How many months or years do you want to put into your education before you start working professionally?
- *Housing options:* If applicable, what kind of housing would you prefer? Dorms, off-campus apartments, and private homes are all common options.
- *Student body:* How would you like the student body to "look"? Think about coed versus all-male and all-female settings, as well as the makeup of minorities, how many students are part-time versus full-time, and the percentage of commuter students.
- *Academic environment:* Consider which majors are offered and at which levels of degree. Research the student-to-faculty ratio. Are the classes taught often by actual professors or more often by the teaching assistants? Find out how many internships the school typically provides to students. Are independent study or study abroad programs available in your area of interest?
- *Financial aid availability/cost:* Does the school provide ample opportunities for scholarships, grants, work-study programs, and the like? Does cost play a role in your options (for most people, it does)?
- *Support services:* Investigate the strength of the academic and career placement counseling services of the school.
- *Social activities and athletics:* Does the school offer clubs that you are interested in? Which sports are offered? Are scholarships available?
- *Specialize programs:* Does the school offer honors programs or programs for veterans or students with disabilities or special needs?

NOTE: Not all of these questions are going to be important to you and that's fine. Be sure to make note of aspects that don't matter so much to you too, such as size or location. You might change your mind as you go to visit colleges, but it's important to make note of where you are to begin with.

U.S. News & World Report[1] puts it best when they say the college that fits you best is one that will do all these things:

- Offer a degree that matches your interests and needs.
- Provide a style of instruction that matches the way you like to learn.

- Provide a level of academic rigor to match your aptitude and preparation.
- Offer a community that feels like home to you.
- Value you for what you do well.

MAKE THE MOST OF CAMPUS VISITS

If it's at all practical and feasible, you should visit the campuses of all the schools you're considering. To get a real feel for any college or university, you need to walk around the campus, spend some time in the common areas where students hang out, and sit in on a few classes. You can also sign up for campus tours, which are typically given by current students. This is another good way to see the campus and ask questions of someone who knows. Be sure to visit the specific school/building that covers your possible major as well. The website and brochures won't be able to convey that intangible feeling you'll get from a visit.

In addition to the questions listed in the previous section in this chapter titled "Finding a Program or School That Fits Your Personality," consider these questions as well. Make a list of questions that are important to you before you visit.

- What is the makeup of the current freshman class? Is the campus diverse?
- What is the meal plan like? What are the food options?
- Where do most of the students hang out between classes? (Be sure to visit this area.)
- How long does it take to walk from one end of the campus to the other?
- What types of transportation are available for students? Does campus security provide escorts to cars, dorms, and so on at night?

To be ready for your visit and make the most of it, consider these tips and words of advice.

Before you go:

- Be sure to do some research. At the least, spend some time on the college website. Make sure your questions aren't addressed adequately there first.
- Make a list of questions.

- Arrange to meet with a professor in your area of interest or to visit the specific school.
- Be prepared to answer questions about yourself and why you are interested in this school.
- Dress in neat, clean, and casual clothes. Avoid overly wrinkled clothing or anything with stains.
- Listen and take notes.
- Don't interrupt.
- Be positive and energetic.
- Make eye contact when someone speaks directly to you.
- Ask questions.
- Thank people for their time.

Finally, be sure to send thank-you notes or emails after the visit is over. Remind the recipient when you visited the campus and thank them for their time.

NOTE: As mentioned previously, given the current coronavirus pandemic, it is possible you will attend many of your courses online. However, many of the points will still apply, such as the student-to-professor ratio and the diversity of the student body.

Hopefully, this section has impressed upon you the importance of finding the right fit for your chosen learning institution. Take some time to paint a mental picture about the kind of university or school setting that will best complement your needs. Then read on for specifics about each degree.

NOTE: In the academic world, accreditation matters and is something you should consider when choosing a school. Accreditation is basically a seal of approval that schools promote to let prospective students feel sure the institution will provide a quality education that is worth the investment and will help graduates reach their career goals. Future employers will want to see that the program you completed has such a seal of quality, so it's something to keep in mind when choosing a school.

Determining Your Education Plan

There are many options, as mentioned, when it comes to pursuing an education in the substance abuse counseling field. These include two-year community colleges, four-year colleges, and masters' programs and PhD programs. This section will focus on undergraduate programs that can help you prepare for your career as a substance abuse counselor.

HOW TO HAVE A GAP YEAR DURING A PANDEMIC

Although a previous section in this chapter explored options for spending a gap year that would certainly offer invaluable experience to an aspiring counselor, unfortunately currently they are not all viable options due to the coronavirus—but that does not mean there aren't enriching activities and pursuits you can engage in to make a gap year just as worthwhile.

Next Advisor[2] offers some tips on how to make the most of a gap year, even if it is not possible to participate in a structured program such as the Peace Corps. Although they may not seem as exciting as traveling abroad, the point of a gap year is to help you refine your interests and gain additional skills before committing yourself to a college program. Here are some options to consider:

- Learn a new skill. Learn a new language. Become an expert in building an online platform if you want to grow your own private practice or reach a broader audience in the future online. Take a photography course. It's a good time to really develop yourself in new areas that may directly or indirectly affect you as a counselor, in that it can help you to look at the world and people differently.
- Read. Science has shown[3] that reading fiction makes us more empathetic, which is a key skill for any counselor (or human, for that matter) to improve.
- Get a job to save money for college. The virus has also hit many hard financially, so taking a year to earn money before heading off to school is certainly a valuable use of your time.
- Volunteer. There are virtual volunteer programs (check out VolunteerMatch) or you can do more local volunteering, such as buying groceries for an elderly neighbor.

- Seek out remote internships. Most people are currently working at home, and there are opportunities for interns to do the same.
- Take online classes at a local community college in a related subject.

Whether you are opting for a two- or four-year degree—and possibly later a master's or even a doctorate—you will find there are many choices. It's a good idea to select roughly five to ten schools in a realistic location (for you) that offer the degree you want to earn. If you are considering online programs, include these in your list.

TIP: Consider attending a university in your resident state, if possible, which will save you lots of money if you attend a state school. Private institutions don't typically discount resident student tuition costs.

Be sure you research the basic GPA and SAT or ACT requirements of each school as well. Although some community colleges do not require standardized tests for the application process, others do.

NOTE: If you are planning to apply to a college or program that requires the ACT or SAT, advisors recommend that students take both the ACT and the SAT tests during their junior year of high school (spring at the latest). You can retake these tests and use your highest score, so be sure to leave time to retake early senior year if needed. You want your best score to be available to all the schools you're applying to by January of your senior year, which will also enable them to be considered with any scholarship applications. Keep in mind these are general timelines; be sure to check the exact deadlines and calendars of the schools to which you're applying!

Once you have found five to ten schools in a realistic location for you that offer the degree you want, spend some time on their websites studying the requirements for admissions. Important factors weighing on your decision of what schools to apply to should include whether you meet the requirements, your chances of getting in (but shoot high!), tuition costs and availability of scholarships and grants, location, and the school's reputation and licensure/ graduation rates.

> NOTE: Most colleges and universities will list the average stats for the last class accepted to the program, which will give you a sense of your chances of acceptance.

The order of these characteristics will depend on your grades and test scores, your financial resources, work experience, and other personal factors. Taking everything into account, you should be able to narrow your list down to the institutes or schools that best match your educational or professional goals as well as your resources and other factors such as location and duration of study.

Schools to Consider When Pursuing a Career as a Substance Abuse Counselor

Some schools and programs have stronger reputations than others. Although you can certainly have a successful and satisfying career and experience without going to the "number-one" school in your field of study, it is a good idea to shop around and to compare different schools and get a sense of what they offer and what features of each are the most important—or least—to you.

> NOTE: According to the Bureau of Labor Statistics,[4] all fifty states require that you earn a specific license before you can work as a substance abuse counselor in a private practice. The requirements for substance abuse counselors not operating a private practice vary by state.

Keep in mind that what is "great" for one person may not be as great for someone else. What might be a perfect school for you might be too difficult, too expensive, or not rigorous enough for someone else. Keep in mind the advice of the previous sections when deciding what you really need in a school.

As mentioned previously, you have a choice of degree type you want to pursue to become qualified as a substance abuse counselor. This section will point you to the best programs for associate, bachelor's, and master's degree programs.

GREAT SCHOOLS FOR SUBSTANCE ABUSE COUNSELING: CERTIFICATE AND ASSOCIATE DEGREE PROGRAMS

The following lists the top online substance abuse counseling certificate and associate degree programs as ranked in 2020 by bestcolleges.com.[5]

> NOTE: States vary when it comes to certification requirements and programs, so you will have to find out what the options and rules are in your state. In California, for example, it is possible to get four levels of substance abuse counseling certifications, which differ in the number of supervised working hours completed in a licensed facility and the level of education already reached, from high school up to a master's degree.

- **City Vision University:** Based in Kansas City, Missouri
- **Bethel University:** Based in Saint Paul, Minnesota
- **Great Basin College:** Based in Elko, Nevada
- **University of Cincinnati:** Based in Cincinnati, Ohio
- **Misericordia University:** Based in Dallas, Pennsylvania
- **Utah Valley University:** Based in Orem, Utah
- **Assumption College:** Based in Worcester, Massachusetts
- **Central Texas College:** Based in Killeen, Texas
- **Albright College:** Based in Reading, Pennsylvania
- **National University:** Based in La Jolla, California

"It excites me to see that the world of mental health overall has become increasingly integrative meaning that settings and the average mental health provider no longer focus just on the mind like they did in the early decades of this profession, but that now we increasingly honor the connection between mind, body, and spirit in how we view psychological wellness."—Kellee Trautmann, LPC, LAC, NCC, licensed professional counselor and licensed addiction counselor

GREAT SCHOOLS FOR SUBSTANCE ABUSE COUNSELING: BACHELOR'S DEGREE PROGRAMS

This list of the best schools offering undergraduate programs in addiction/substance abuse counseling—from number one to number ten—has been compiled by CollegeChoice.net.[6]

- **University of Cincinnati:** Based in Cincinnati, Ohio
- **Indiana Wesleyan University:** Based in Marion, Indiana
- **Drexel University:** Based in Philadelphia, Pennsylvania
- **Northwestern State University of Louisiana:** Based in Natchitoches, Louisiana
- **University of South Dakota:** Based in Vermillion, South Dakota
- **SUNY College Brockport:** Based in Brockport, New York
- **University of Detroit, Mercy:** Based in Detroit, Michigan
- **Alvernia University:** Based in Reading, Pennsylvania
- **University of St. Francis:** Based in Joliet, Illinois
- **Keene State College:** Based in Keene, New Hampshire

GREAT SCHOOLS FOR SUBSTANCE ABUSE COUNSELING: MASTER'S DEGREE PROGRAMS

Although there are on-campus master's programs in substance abuse counseling, many people who already hold a bachelor's degree and are thinking about earning a master's choose to do so while they are working. Many of the best master's programs are available to follow online, which means you don't have to relocate and you can continue working while earning your degree if you choose. You can often earn your degree part time to make this possible. Here are the top ten schools offering such master's programs, according to TheBest Schools.org.

- **Governors State University:** Based in University Park, Illinois
- **West Virginia University:** Based in Morgantown, West Virginia
- **University of South Dakota:** Based in Vermillion, South Dakota
- **Liberty University:** Based in Lynchburg, Virginia
- **Nova Southeastern University:** Based in Fort Lauderdale, Florida
- **Regent University:** Based in Virginia Beach, Virginia
- **Virginia Commonwealth University:** Based in Richmond, Virginia
- **University of the Cumberlands:** Based in Williamsburg, Kentucky
- **Wright State University:** Based in Bath Township, Ohio
- **Washburn University:** Based in Topeka, Kansas

What's It Going to Cost You?

So, the bottom line: What will your education end up costing you? First, some good news: According to *U.S. News and World Report*, the average tuition costs for colleges fell in 2020, which went against the standard trend of cost going up each year. For private colleges, costs fell by about 5 percent; for in-state colleges, the costs fell by 4 percent; and for out-of-state (tuition for a person attending a state school but not in their resident state) the costs have fallen by 6 percent.[7]

NOTE: Also according to *U.S. News and World Report*,[8] the cost of an out-of-state school compared with an in-state school is 72 percent higher, so looking for a school in the state in which you are registered is definitely a way to cut down the costs of your education.

This trend appears to be continuing, according to an update by *U.S. News and World Report*[9] that looks at tuition rates for the 2021–2022 school year. This comes amid some calls for a tuition discount, as the coronavirus disease pandemic has forced so many institutions to move to online course delivery.

In addition, there are several financial aid options to help you find the funding to earn the degree you want. We cover those next.

School can be an expensive investment, but there are many ways to seek help paying for your education.
designer491/iStock/Getty Images

WRITING A GREAT PERSONAL STATEMENT FOR ADMISSION

The personal statement you include with your application to college is extremely important, especially when your GPA and SAT/ACT scores are on the border of what is typically accepted. Write something that is thoughtful and conveys your understanding of the profession you are interested in, as well as your desire to practice in this field. Why are you uniquely qualified? Why are you a good fit for this university? These essays should be highly personal (the "personal" in personal statement). Will the admissions professionals who read it, along with hundreds of others, come away with a snapshot of who you really are and what you are passionate about?

Look online for some examples of good ones, which will give you a feel for what works. Be sure to check your specific school for length guidelines, format requirements, and any other guidelines they expect you to follow.

And of course, be sure to proofread it several times and ask a professional (such as your school writing center or your local library services) to proofread it as well.

Financial Aid: Finding Money for Education

Finding the money to attend college can seem out of reach. But you can do it if you have a plan before you actually start applying to college. If you get into your top-choice university, don't let the sticker cost turn you away. Financial aid can come from many different sources and it's available to cover all different kinds of costs you'll encounter during your years in college, including tuition, fees, books, housing, and food.

The good news is that universities more often offer incentive or tuition discount aid to encourage students to attend. The market is often more competitive in favor of the student, and colleges and universities are responding by offering more generous aid packages to a wider range of students than they used to. Here are some basic tips and pointers about the financial aid process:

- You apply for financial aid during your senior year. You must fill out the Free Application for Federal Student Aid (FAFSA) form at studentaid .gov, which can be filed starting October 1 of your senior year until June of the year you graduate. Because the amount of available aid is limited, it's best to apply as soon as you possibly can. See fafsa.gov to get started.

- Be sure to compare and contrast deals you get at different schools. There is room to negotiate with universities. The first offer for aid may not be the best you'll get.
- Wait until you receive all offers from your top schools and then use this information to negotiate with your top choice to see if they will match or beat the best aid package you received.
- To be eligible to keep and maintain your financial aid package, you must meet certain grade/GPA requirements. Be sure you are clear on these academic expectations and keep up with them.
- You must reapply for federal aid every year.

NOTE: Watch out for scholarship scams! You should never be asked to pay to submit the FAFSA form ("free" is in its name) or be required to pay a lot to find appropriate aid and scholarships. These are free services. If an organization promises you you'll get aid or that you have to "act now or miss out," these are both warning signs of a less reputable organization.

Also be careful with your personal information to avoid identity theft as well. Simple things like closing and exiting your browser after visiting sites where you entered personal information. Don't share your student aid ID number with anyone either.

It's important to understand the different forms of financial aid that are available to you. That way, you'll know how to apply for different kinds and get the best financial aid package that fits your needs and strengths. The two main categories that financial aid falls under are *gift aid*, which don't have to be repaid, and *self-help aid*, which are either loans that must be repaid or work-study funds that are earned. The next sections cover the various types of financial aid that fit in one of these areas.

GRANTS

Grants typically are awarded to students who have financial needs but can also be used in the areas of athletics, academics, demographics, veteran support, and special talents. They do not have to be paid back. Grants can come from federal agencies, state agencies, specific universities, and private organizations. Most federal and state grants are based on financial need.

Examples of grants are the Pell Grant, SMART Grant, and the Federal Supplemental Educational Opportunity Grant (FSEOG). Visit the US Department of Education's federal student aid site for lots of current information about grants (see https://studentaid.ed.gov/types/grants-scholarships).

SCHOLARSHIPS

Scholarships are merit-based aid that does not have to be paid back. They are typically awarded based on academic excellence or some other special talent, such as music or art. Scholarships also fall under the areas of athletic-based, minority-based, aid for women, and so forth. These are typically not awarded by federal or state governments but instead come from the specific university applied to as well as private and nonprofit organizations.

Be sure to reach out directly to the financial aid officers of the schools you want to attend. These people are great contacts that can lead you to many more sources of scholarships and financial aid. Visit http://www.gocollege.com/financial-aid/scholarships/types/ for lots more information about how scholarships in general work.

LOANS

Many types of loans are available, especially to students, to pay for their postsecondary education. However, the important thing to remember here is that loans must be paid back, with interest. Be sure you understand the interest rate you will be charged. This is the extra cost of borrowing the money and is usually a percentage of the amount you borrow. Is this fixed or will it change over time? Is the loan and interest deferred until you graduate (meaning you don't have to begin paying it off until after you graduate)? Is the loan subsidized (meaning the federal government pays the interest until you graduate)? These are all points you need to be clear about before you sign on the dotted line.

There are many types of loans offered to students, including need-based loans, non-need-based loans, state loans, and private loans. Two reputable federal loans are the Perkins Loan and the Direct Stafford Loan. For more information about student loans, start at https://bigfuture.collegeboard.org/pay-for-college/loans/types-of-college-loans.

FEDERAL WORK-STUDY

The US federal work-study program provides part-time jobs for undergraduate and graduate students with financial need so they can earn money to pay for educational expenses. The focus of such work is on community service work and work related to a student's course of study. Not all colleges and universities participate in this program, so be sure to check with the school financial aid office if this is something you are counting on. The sooner you apply, the more likely you will get the job you desire and be able to benefit from the program because funds are limited. See https://studentaid.ed.gov/sa/types/work-study for more information about this opportunity.

MEANINGFUL CONNECTIONS

Joy Koczka.
Courtesy of Joy Koczka.

Joy Koczka, RSW, MSW, BSW, BA, is a mental health therapist who has worked with individuals struggling with substance use issues for several years. Joy began her career as a social worker then obtained a master's degree in clinical social work in 2012. Since that time, Joy has been a therapist working in various capacities with both youth and adults and specialized in dialectical behavior therapy (DBT) in her master's program whereby she developed a manual for delivering DBT with youth as well as a youth workbook. Joy has trained colleagues in the DBT approach as well as in trauma and attachment. Throughout her career she has worked with many individuals struggling with substance use. She is currently a therapist at Quest Health Inc. where she facilitates DBT group therapy and individual therapy with Indigenous populations, many of which struggle with substance abuse.

How is substance abuse counseling part of your role as a therapist?

As a therapist working within the mental health field, you often find that these individuals also struggle with substance use problems. The use of substances is often part of an individual's attempt to cope with the emotional issues whether it be anxiety, depression, post-traumatic stress disorder (PTSD), or any mental health issue. Unfortunately, the continued use of substances oftentimes becomes an addiction. As a therapist I see addiction as a disease but also view it as a symptom of a deeper emotional problem. In my work, I have found that many people who struggle with addiction issues have experienced trauma in their life. I think it is essential that in order to help a client create meaningful change in their lives we must address the underlying emotional issues they are struggling with. I believe that no matter what stage that individual is in in terms of their substance use they deserve to be treated with dignity and respect. We need to start with "where the client is at," whether or not they are ready to address their substance use issues. I think professionals working with individuals with substance use issues need to consider the merit of "harm reduction" strategies not only "abstinence" from substances.

Can you describe your educational background and career path to date?

I started off my career with a bachelor's in social work (BSW) and worked as a medical social worker and child and family services (CFS) worker. While obtaining my master's degree in clinical social work (MSW), I worked as a crisis clinician for youth mobile crisis in Winnipeg. Upon obtaining my MSW I worked as a therapist for several years at Knowles Centre which is a treatment center for youth with substantial emotional and behavioral issues as well as a therapist for MacDonald Youth Services working with even more pronounced emotional and behavioral issues in youth. During this time I also facilitated DBT group therapy with these youth. From there I went on to develop my own private practice and worked as a therapist for Blue Cross. I am currently a therapist for Quest Health Inc. where I facilitate DBT group therapy and provide individual therapy with Indigenous people. Throughout my whole career I have worked with individuals struggling with substance use issues.

What is a typical day on the job for you?

My job is two-fold; I spend two weeks of the month (Monday to Friday) facilitating DBT group therapy with Indigenous people, many of whom struggle with substance use issues. The other two weeks I travel to Indigenous communities and provide individual therapy.

What's the best or most satisfying part of your job?

I would say one of the most satisfying parts of my job is when I know I have made a meaningful connection with my client. I think developing a trusting relationship with your client is integral to helping them, without that you will not get anywhere in terms of helping them. The other satisfying part is when they thank me for the help I have given to them and when I believe that I have made a difference in their lives.

What's the most challenging part or stressful part of your job?

I think the most challenging part of my job is working against the systemic oppressive structures that exist for Indigenous people. My clients have experienced so much oppression in their lives stemming from the colonization of Indigenous people. As a result, these individuals have experienced intergenerational trauma. Something that did not need to happen, happened and has caused so much damage to these individuals and is responsible for the many struggles they have today.

What has been the most surprising thing about your job working as a therapist working with individuals who have substance abuse issues?

I would say the most surprising thing is the resilience that my clients have. I try as a therapist to "put myself in their shoes" and I am forever struck by their strength and willingness to keep trying.

What kinds of qualities do you consider advantageous to doing your job successfully?

There are many qualities that are essential to doing this type of work successfully. Not thinking of yourself as the "expert" in your clients' lives is essential. They are the "experts" in their own lives and it is important that therapy is done in a way that promotes an equal relationship between the therapist and client. Being nonjudgmental is also an essential quality. Being able to self-reflect and take a good look at yourself is integral and recognizing your own biases and challenging them because well all have them and if we do not do this it will have a negative effect on our work. Never thinking you know everything and having an open mind to new ideas and perspectives are essential. I am constantly learning and trying to improve my skills as a therapist and I learn from my clients all the time.

How do you combat burnout?

Combating burnout is something you need to do all the time. How I do this is by putting things into perspective. What we do is hard and we are working with individuals who have it the hardest so it helps me to remember that there are people out there who are not struggling as badly. Having balance is extremely important.

There is more to life than your job so we need to remember that and try to have a life outside of work and know your limits. Self-care is important and that could mean different things for different people. For me I know I am not taking care of myself when I am not sleeping enough, not eating as healthy as I should, and not taking the time to enjoy the company of friends and family. Being able to debrief with a colleague who does the same work you do is important. Using debriefing as a way to validate your own challenges and feelings as well as consulting regarding your work can go a long way to combat burnout.

How do you see your career or the substance abuse field evolving in the future?

I think the substance abuse field is currently evolving. The "harm reduction" approach to substance abuse is an evolving field. This means recognizing that abstinence from substances may not be possible for some people given the stage of change that they are in with their struggle against substances. Programs such as "managed alcohol programs" is but one example whereby individuals can slowly cut down on their substance use and not suffer from severe withdrawal. We must also recognize that "conventional treatment programs" do not always work for some people and that there are many ways to recover. Cultural healing practices are one of these examples. Some people can recover and heal from substance abuse on their own and do not require the help of a substance abuse counselor so recognizing that treatment or counseling is not always the answer for some people.

Summary

This chapter covered all the aspects of college and postsecondary schooling that you'll want to consider as you move forward. Remember that finding the right fit is especially important because it increases the chances that you'll stay in school and earn your degree, as well as have an amazing experience while you're at it.

In this chapter, we discussed how to evaluate and compare your options to get the best education for the best deal. You also learned a little about scholarships and financial aid, how the SAT and ACT tests work, if applicable, and how to write a unique personal statement that eloquently expresses your passions.

Use this chapter as a jumping off point to dig deeper into your particular area of interest. Some tidbits of wisdom to leave you with:

- Take the SAT and ACT tests early in your junior year so you have time to take them again. Most universities automatically accept the highest scores.
- Make sure that the institution you plan to attend has an accredited program in your field of study. Some professions follow national accreditation policies, while others are state-mandated and, therefore, differ across state lines. Do your research and understand the differences.
- Don't underestimate how important campus visits are, especially in the pursuit of finding the right academic fit. Come prepared to ask questions not addressed on the school website or in the literature.
- Your personal statement is an important piece of your application that can set you apart from others. Take the time and energy needed to make it unique and compelling.
- Don't assume you can't afford a school based on the "sticker price." Many schools offer great scholarships and aid to qualified students. It doesn't hurt to apply. This advice especially applies to minorities, veterans, and students with disabilities.
- Don't lose sight of the fact that it's important to pursue a career that you enjoy, are good at, and are passionate about! You'll be a happier person if you do so.

At this point, your career goals and aspirations should be gelling. At the least, you should have a plan for finding out more information. Remember to do the research about the university, school, or degree program before you reach out and especially before you visit. Faculty and staff find students who ask challenging questions much more impressive than those who ask questions that can be answered by spending ten minutes on the school website.

In chapter 4, we go into detail about the next steps—writing a résumé and cover letter, interviewing well, follow-up communications, and more. This is information you can use to secure internships, volunteer positions, summer jobs, and more. It's not just for college grads. In fact, the sooner you can hone these communication skills, the better off you'll be in the professional world.

4

Writing Your Résumé and Interviewing

With each chapter of this book, we have narrowed the process from the broadest of strokes—what substance abuse counselors do—to how to plan your strategy and educational approach to making your dream job a reality.

In this chapter, we will cover the steps involved in applying for jobs or schools: how to prepare an effective résumé and slam-dunk an interview. Your résumé is your opportunity to summarize your experience, training, education, and goals and attract employers or school administrators. The goal of the résumé is to land the interview, and the goal of the interview is to land the job. Even if you do not have much working experience, you can still put together a résumé that expresses your interests and goals and the activities that illustrate your competence and interest.

As well as a résumé, you will be expected to write a cover letter that is basically your opportunity to reveal a little bit more about your passion, your motivation for a job or educational opportunity, and often to express more about you personally to give a potential employer a sense of who you are and what drives you. And particularly because you are striving for a career in a competitive and passion-based field, and one in which your success will rely on personal characteristics as well as academic credentials, it's wise to ensure your uniqueness, motivation, and commitment for working toward a meaningful cause—whatever your goal—comes through.

Giving the right impression is undoubtedly important, but don't let that make you nervous. In a résumé, cover letter, or interview, you want to put forward your best but your genuine self. Dress professionally, proofread carefully (especially as you are applying to a job in the writing sphere!), but ensure you are being yourself. In this chapter, we will cover all of these important aspects of the job-hunting process, and by the end, you will feel confident and ready to present yourself as a candidate for the job you really want.

Writing Your Résumé

Writing your first résumé can feel challenging because you have likely not yet gained a lot of experience in a professional setting. But don't fret; employers understand that you are new to the workforce or to the particular career you are seeking. The right approach is never to exaggerate or invent experience or accomplishments but to present yourself as someone with a good work ethic, a genuine interest in the particular job or organization, and use what you can to present yourself authentically and honestly.

There are some standard elements to an effective résumé that you should be sure to include. At the top should be your name, of course, as well as email address or other contact information. Always list your experience in chronological order, beginning with your current or most recent position—or whatever experience you want to share.

NOTE: Although résumés for any job all contain similar types of information presented in a similar structure, for a counselor role, it's a good idea to stress personal attributes that lend themselves especially to the job. MyPerfectResume.com[1] particularly recommends that aspiring substance abuse counselors should stress their compassion for people and desire to help others of "all socioeconomic and cultural backgrounds." Your résumé should also highlight any certifications you hold in addition to college degrees, your knowledge of drug types, and clinical experiences as they relate to the job.

If you are a recent graduate with little work experience, begin with your education. If you've been in the working world for a while, you can opt to list your education or any certification you have at the end. List anywhere you have been published and any published work you may have edited.

NOTE: You may need to customize your résumé for different purposes to ensure you are not filling it with information that does not directly link to your qualifications for a particular job.

If this is your first résumé, be sure you highlight your education where you can—any courses you've taken be it in high school or through a community college or any other place that offers training related to your job target. Also highlight any hobbies or volunteer experience you have. But be concise; one page is usually appropriate, especially for your first résumé.

TIP: Before preparing your résumé, try to connect with a hiring professional—a human resources person or hiring manager—in a similar position or organization you are interested in. They can give you advice on what employees look for and what information to highlight on your résumé, as well as what types of interview questions you can expect.

As important as your résumé's content is the way you design and format it. You can find several samples online of résumés that you can be inspired by—some specifically for substance abuse counselors, such as at LiveCareer.com[2] or Job Hero.[3] At TheBalanceCareers.com,[4] for example, you can find many templates and design ideas. You want your résumé to be attractive to the eye and formatted in a way that makes the key points easy to spot and digest; according to some research, employees take an average of six seconds to review a résumé, so you don't have a lot of time to get across your experience and value.

LINKING-IN WITH IMPACT

As well as your paper or electronic résumé, creating a LinkedIn profile is a good way to highlight your experience and promote yourself, as well as to network. Joining professional organizations or connecting with other people in your desired field are good ways to keep abreast of changes and trends and work opportunities.

The key elements of a LinkedIn profile are your photo, your headline, and your profile summary. These are the most revealing parts of the profile, and the ones employers and connections will base their impression of you on.

The photo should be carefully chosen. Remember that LinkedIn is not Facebook or Instagram; it is not the place to share a photo of you acting too casually on vacation or at a party. According to Joshua Waldman, author of *Job Searching with*

Social Media for Dummies,[5] the choice of photo should be taken seriously and be done right. His tips:

- Choose a photo in which you have a nice smile.
- Dress in professional clothing.
- Ensure the background of the photo is pleasing to the eye. According to Waldman, some colors—like green and blue—convey a feeling of trust and stability.
- Remember it's not a mug shot. You can be creative with the angle of your photo rather than stare directly into the camera.
- Use your photo to convey some aspect of your personality.
- Focus on your face. Remember visitors to your profile will see only a small thumbnail image, so be sure your face takes up most of it.

The important thing is to present the most important and relevant information at the top. Your résumé needs to be as easy to navigate and read.

WRITING AN OBJECTIVE

The objective section of your résumé is one of the most important because it is the first section a recruiter or hiring manager will read and, therefore, the first sense they will develop of you as a candidate. The objective should be brief but poignant. Definitely it should be focused and give a sense of you as a unique applicant—you don't want it to be generic or bland—show how creative you can be while keeping it professional. It's important to take your time and really refine your objective so you can stand out and attract employers or clients.

Be sure you do your research about what the job and the organization to which you are applying. Know exactly what kind of counselor the organization is looking for. Then you can better craft your objective to highlight the ways in which you uniquely match their needs.

"I see addiction as a disease but also view it as a symptom of a deeper emotional problem. In my work, I have found that many people who struggle with addiction issues have experienced trauma in their life. I think it is essential that in order to help a client create meaningful change in their lives we must address the underlying emotional issues they are struggling with."—Joy Koczka, RSW, MSW, BSW, BA, is a mental health therapist

Writing Your Cover Letter

As well as your résumé, most employers will ask that you submit a cover letter. This is a one-page letter in which you express your motivation, why you are interested in the organization or position, and what skills you possess that make you the right fit.

Here are some tips for writing an effective cover letter:

- As always, proofread your text carefully before submitting it.
- Be sure you have a letter that is focused on a specific job. Do not make it too general or one-size-fits-all. Your personality and uniqueness should come through, or the recruiter or hiring manager will move on to the next application.
- Summarize why you are right for the position. Keep it relevant and specific to what the particular organization is looking for in a candidate and employee.
- Keep your letter to one page whenever possible.
- Introduce yourself in a way that makes the reader want to know more about you, and encourage them to review your résumé.
- Be specific about the job you are applying for. Mention the title and be sure it is correct.
- Try to find the name of the person who will receive your letter rather than keeping it nonspecific ("to whom it may concern").
- Be sure you include your contact details.
- End with a "call to action"—a request for an interview, for example.

Interviewing Skills

With your sparkling résumé, LinkedIn profile, and cover letter, you are bound to be called for an interview. This is an important stage to reach: You will have already gone through several filters; a potential employer has gotten a quick scan of your experience and has reviewed your LinkedIn profile and has made the decision to learn more about you in person.

There's no way to know ahead of time exactly what to expect in an interview, but there are many ways to prepare yourself. You can start by learning more about the person who will be interviewing you. In the same way recruiters and employers can learn about you online, you can do the same. You can see if you have any education or work experience in common or any contacts you both know. It's perfectly acceptable and even considered proactive in a positive way to research the person with whom you'll be interviewing, such as on LinkedIn.

Be it in person or via video call, a job interview can be stressful. You can help calm your nerves and feel more confident if you prepare ahead by thinking about answers to questions you can anticipate being asked.
Inside Creative House/iStock/Getty Images

Preparing yourself for the types of questions you will be asked to ensure you offer a thoughtful and meaningful response is vital to interview success. Particularly when you are applying for a job that will require and depend on how you present yourself conversationally, it is paramount that you respond in an effective, composed manner. Consider your answers carefully, and be prepared to support them with examples and anecdotes.

Here are some questions you should be prepared to be asked. It's a good idea to consider your answers carefully, without memorizing what you mean to say (because that can throw you off and will be obvious to the interviewer). Think carefully about your responses and be prepared to deliver them in a natural manner.

- Why did you decide to enter this field? What drives your passion for working in the counseling industry?
- What is your educational background? What credentials did you earn?
- What counseling experience do you have?
- Are you a team player? Describe your usual role in a team-centered work environment. Do you easily assume a leadership role?

BEWARE WHAT YOU SHARE ON SOCIAL MEDIA

Most of us engage in social media. Sites such as Facebook, Twitter, and Instagram provide us a platform for sharing photos and memories, opinions, and life events, and reveal everything from our political stance to our sense of humor. It's a great way to connect with people around the world, but once you post something, it's accessible to anyone—including potential employers—unless you take mindful precaution.

Your posts may be public, which means you may be making the wrong impression without realizing it. More and more, people are using search engines like Google to get a sense of potential employers, colleagues, or employees, and the impression you make online can have a strong impact on how you are perceived. Approximately 70 percent of employers[6] search for information on candidates on social media sites.

Glassdoor.com[7] offers the following tips for how to avoid your social media activity from sabotaging your career success:

1. Check your privacy settings. Ensure that your photos and posts are only accessible to the friends or contacts you want to see them. You want to come across as professional and reliable.

2. Rather than avoid social media while searching for a job, use it to your advantage. It's to your advantage to have an online presence (as long as it's a flattering one). Give future employees a sense of your professional interest by "liking" pages or joining groups of professional organizations related to your career goals.

3. Grammar counts. Be attentive to the quality of writing of all your posts and comments.

4. Be consistent. With each social media outlet, there is a different focus and tone of what you are communicating. LinkedIn is professional, while Facebook is far more social and relaxed. It's okay to take a different tone on various social media sites, but be sure you aren't blatantly contradicting yourself.

5. Choose your username carefully. Remember, social media may be the first impression anyone has of you in the professional realm.

Dressing Appropriately

How you dress for a job interview is important to the impression you want to make. Remember that the interview, no matter what the actual environment in which you'd be working, is your chance to present your most professional self. Although you will not likely ever wear a suit to work, for the interview it's the most professional choice.

TIP: A suit is no longer an absolute requirement in many job interviews but avoid looking too casual as it will give the impression you are not that interested.

What Employers Expect

Hiring managers and human resource professionals will also have certain expectations of you at an interview. The main thing is preparation; it cannot be overstated that you should arrive to an interview appropriately dressed, on time, unhurried, and ready to answer—and ask—questions.

For any job interview, the main things employers will look for are that you

- Have a thorough understanding of the organization and the job for which you are applying.
- Be prepared to answer questions about yourself and your relevant experience.
- Be poised and likeable but still professional. They will be looking for a sense of what it would be like to work with you on a daily basis and how your presence would fit in the culture of the business.
- Stay engaged. Listen carefully to what is being asked and offer thoughtful but concise answers. Don't blurt out answers you've memorized but really focus on what is being asked.
- Be prepared to ask your own questions. It shows how much you understand the flow of an organization or workplace and how you will contribute to it. Some questions you can ask:
  - What created the need to fill this position? Is it a new position or has someone left the organization?
  - Where does this position fit in the overall hierarchy of the organization?
  - What are the key skills required to succeed in this job?
  - What challenges might I expect to face within the first six months on the job?
  - How does this position relate to the achievement of the organization's (or department's, or boss's) goals?
  - How would you describe the organization's culture?

THERAPISTS SHOULD BE SELF-AWARE

Kellee Trautmann, LPC, LAC, NCC, is a Licensed Professional Counselor and Licensed Addiction Counselor who owns a private practice in Longmont, Colorado. She provides individual counseling and group therapy both virtually and in person to adults ages twenty-five to fifty-five. She specializes in working with the LGBTQ+

Kellee Trautmann.
Courtesy of Kellee Trautmann.

community, minorities, and trauma survivors using strengths-based approaches that focus on attachment neurobiology to guide her clients through recovery from anxiety, obsessive-compulsive disorder, and substance use disorders and to celebrate healing worth braving!

How did you choose substance abuse counseling as a career?

Admittedly I had not set out from the beginning of my post–high school career to become an addiction counselor, though I did have it in my heart since high school to become a counselor. It was the combination of my lifelong interest in cultural similarities and differences, curiosity about what makes us who we are, and my value of helping others that inspired my interest in psychology. It wasn't until my late twenties when I was in the middle of my Master's in Counseling program that I decided to gain additional educational and job experience related to helping others navigate through addiction and recovery. It was out of a realization addiction impacts every single family in one way or another that made me want to feel as equipped as possible to guide others in this area and I have no regrets!

Can you describe your educational background and career path to date?

The combination of a lifelong curiosity in cultural differences, human behavior, and peoples' resilience led me to pursue a bachelor's degree in psychology and French during which time I was able to study abroad for one semester in France. After graduating college my love of the mountains led me to move to Colorado. While I always thought I would attend graduate school directly after college, I ended up working for a few years getting relevant experience by working as a case manager. As a case manager I was able to help those impacted by severe mental illness to gain access to resources in their home such as assistance with cooking and cleaning. I then completed a four-year master of arts program in Multicultural Clinical Mental Health Counseling at the University of Colorado Denver during which time I worked various part-time jobs gaining further applied experience.

After graduate school I worked as a counselor in residential addiction recovery programs where clients lived and received treatment for an average of ninety days. This allowed me to collect the three thousand clinical hours that were needed in order to become licensed as both a Licensed Professional Counselor and a Licensed Addiction's Counselor, both of which can provide talk therapy. I then started my own business, Wild Transformations Therapy, a solo business in which I am the only employee.

What is a typical day on the job for you?

A typical day of mine involves seeing approximately six clients each for fifty-minute sessions. In between sessions I am often completing paperwork to document the sessions which is a requirement as a counselor. If I am not doing paperwork I am responding to emails of clients who need to reschedule, responding to calls of new clients who are interested in starting therapy, attending educational or marketing events at recovery centers in order to have other clinicians who I can refer community members to when I don't have openings for new clients, or making brief calls to my clients' other providers such as their psychiatrist to collaborate care.

What's the best or most satisfying part of your job?

The most satisfying part of my job is definitely being able to witness positive change over time in people and getting to see the look of pride on their face when they realize, usually a few months into therapy, that all the small actions they have taken have added up to living a life more in line with their values. Since I often work with people who are survivors of trauma of various kinds including having grown up in addicted families, the goal is not always behavior change but grieving the childhood they did not have. In these cases, it is very rewarding to witness when clients come to realize that what has happened to them is not their fault and does not make them fundamentally bad, but rather fundamentally worthy of safe love!

What's the most challenging part or stressful part of your job?

As someone who always wants to know I'm doing a good job the most challenging part of my career is the ambiguity. Change and healing are very ambiguous processes that are not neatly quantifiable or measurable. This requires trusting yourself at the end of each day that you responded in helpful ways and this part becomes easier over time. It is also very difficult to lose clients to suicide and addiction which makes it important to have a group of colleagues and friends who are counselors for support and understanding during these times.

What kinds of qualities and personal characteristics do you consider advantageous to doing your job successfully?

Persistence and grit were really helpful to have during college and graduate school in order to become a therapist. It is not about being the smartest person in the room, but more important to not burn out and be able to balance high levels of expectation and homework for long periods of time with fun and spending time with those you love. It is equivalent to running a marathon and taking breaks as opposed to trying to sprint. Being self-aware is also an immensely helpful attribute to have as a therapist.

How do you combat burnout?

I think one of the most important things is to have a group of close friends and a hobby you enjoy that you can do at the end of the day that has nothing to do with helping others. For me, I enjoy doing yoga, cooking, and spending time with my fiancé and two cats! Since I live in Colorado when it's nice out I enjoy hiking, even if it's a long walk around town.

How do you see your career or the substance abuse field evolving in the future?

It excites me to see that the world of mental health overall has become increasingly integrative, meaning that settings and the average mental health provider no longer focus just on the mind like they did in the early decades of this profession, but that now we increasingly honor the connection between mind, body, and spirit in how we view psychological wellness. I think we will increasingly see centers that have physical healthcare, counseling, and access to services such as massage, acupuncture, yoga, and nutrition all in the same place!

Summary

Congratulations on working through the book! You should now have a strong idea of your career goals within the substance abuse counseling field and how to realize them. In this chapter, we covered how to present yourself as the right candidate to a potential employer, and these strategies are also relevant if you are applying to a college or another form of training.

Here are some tips to sum it up:

- Your résumé should be concise and focused on only relevant aspects of your work experience or education. Although you can include some personal hobbies or details, they should be related to the job and your qualifications for it.

- Take your time with all your professional documents—your résumé, you cover letter, your LinkedIn profile—and be sure to proofread carefully to avoid embarrassing and sloppy mistakes.
- Prepare yourself for an interview but anticipating the types of questions you will be asked and coming up with professional and meaningful responses.
- Equally, prepare some questions for your potential employer to ask at the interview. This will show you have a good understanding and interest in the organization and what role you would have in it.
- Always follow up after an interview with a letter or an email. An email is the fastest way to express your gratitude for the interviewer's time and restate your interest in the position.
- Dress appropriately for an interview and pay extra attention to tidiness and hygiene.
- Be wary of what you share on social media sites while job searching. Most employers research candidates online and what you have shared will influence their idea of who you are and what it would be like to work with you.

You've chosen to pursue a career in a competitive, challenging, but also broad and exciting field. We wish you great success in your future.

Further Resources

The following websites, magazines, and organizations can help you further investigate and educate yourself on substance abuse counselor topics, all of which will help you as you take the next steps in your career, now and throughout your professional life.

Publications and Websites

Addiction Professional
www.psychcongress.com/node/720
A clinical magazine for those who work in the field of addiction recovery that provides insights and contributions from a wide range of writers and editors.

Counselor
https://thecreativeindependent.com/guides/how-to-write-a-book-proposal/
One of the most reputable and well-known magazines for addiction professionals.

Counselor Magazine
counselormagazine.com
A print and online publication dedicated to the publishing and editing industry. The official publication of the California Association of Addiction Programs and Professionals (CCAPP).

Renew Magazine
http://reneweveryday.com/
A magazine for professionals who want to stay updated on the latest news impacting the addiction recovery field.

Treatment Magazine

treatmentmagazine.com

A magazine that provides information, resources, support, community, and positive stories for everyone who seeks treatment.

Blogs

An Addict in Our Son's Bedroom

http://parentsofanaddict.blogspot.com/

A drug addiction blog that is a great resource for family members or friends of an addict.

Addiction Recovery

https://www.recoveryconnection.com/addiction-recovery-blog/

A "safe and non-triggering" addiction recovery blog for the recovery community.

Addiction & Recovery News

https://addictionandrecoverynews.wordpress.com/

Focuses on the stigma, media coverage, and research surrounding drug and alcohol addiction.

The Fix

www.thefix.com

A recovery blog offering different perspectives on addiction from a number of authors, including personal accounts and expert voices.

A Hangover Free Life

https://ahangoverfreelife.com/

Lucy offers personal stories about overcoming addiction and staying sober.

Hip Sobriety

https://www.hipsobriety.com/

Holly Glen Whitaker shares her story and shows that anybody can suffer from addiction.

Mrs. D Is Going Without

http://livingwithoutalcohol.blogspot.com/

A blog that chronicles the experiences of the early stages of sobriety, from the personal life of its author who is living without alcohol.

She Recovers

https://sherecovers.org/blog/

A blog focused on alcohol abuse recovery that also provides information on webinars and other sources of information.

Sober Living

www.soberjulie.com

Provides information and tips on staying sober when attending social events or going on holiday.

The Sobriety Collective

www.thesobrietycollective.com

A popular and well regarded sobriety blog run by Laura. A welcoming place that takes the stigma out of addiction.

Glossary

acupuncture: A treatment that entails inserting small needles into a patient to promote healing.

Alcohol Anonymous (AA): An international organization with the stated purpose of enabling its members to stay sober and help other alcoholics achieve sobriety.

associate degree: A four-year degree awarded by a college or university.

bachelor's degree: A four-year degree awarded by a college or university.

behavioral science: The study of human or animal behavior.

behavioral therapies: Therapies that focus on guiding a client to understand the root causes of destructive, high-risk behaviors.

brief strategic family therapy: Therapy that addresses family interactions on issues that make teens particularly vulnerable to substance abuse, such as difficulties at school or with peer groups.

burnout: Feeling of physical and emotional exhaustion caused by overworking.

campus: The location of a school, college, or university.

career assessment test: A test that asks questions particularly geared to identify skills and interests to help inform test takers on what type of career would suit them.

cognitive behavioral therapy (CBT): Therapy that helps clients anticipate situations that are high-risk for prompting substance abuse.

colleagues: The people with whom people work.

community college: A two-year college that awards associate's degrees.

community reinforcement: A rewards-based system that typically involves twenty-four therapy sessions with an emphasis on developing new hobbies, strengthening and improving relationships, and growing and deepening social support.

contingency management and motivational incentives: An award-system therapy of sorts, in which positive behavior is "reinforced" with concrete rewards—such as vouchers for retail goods and events like movie tickets in exchange for "clean" drug tests.

counselor: A qualified person who counsels or advises a person through a difficult problem.

cover letter: A document that usually accompanies a résumé and allows candidates applying to a job or a school or internship an opportunity to describe their motivation and qualifications.

dialectical behavior therapy (DBT): This type of therapy focuses on relaxation practices such as yoga and controlled-breathing exercises to help improve focus and calm.

educational background: The degrees a person has earned and schools attended.

empathy: The quality of being able to understand the feelings of another person.

eye movement desensitization and reprocessing (EMDR): Therapy that helps a person to reprocess a memory of a traumatizing event so its negative impact can be reduced and the person can heal.

family behavior therapy: Therapy that aims to address how the family as a complete unit has been impacted by substance abuse, trauma, or some other problem.

financial aid: Various means of receiving financial support for the purposes of attending school. This can be a grant or scholarship, for example.

gap year: A year between high school and higher education or employment during which a person can explore passions and interests, often while traveling.

General Education Development (GED) degree: A degree that is the equivalent to a high school diploma without graduating from high school.

holistic therapy: Therapy that aims to achieve optimal health and wellness by aligning all parts of a person, including their body, mind, spirit, and emotions.

homeless: A person who does not have a permanent place of residence; also referred to as *unhomed*.

in-state school: A nonprivate college that exists in the state in which a person is a resident. In-state schools offer lower tuitions to state residents.

industry: The people and activities involved in one type of business, such as the business of publishing.

internship: A work experience opportunity that lasts for a set period of time and can be paid or unpaid.

interpersonal skills: The ability to communicate and interact with other people in an effective manner.

interviewing: A part of the job-seeking process in which a candidate meets with a potential employer, usually face-to-face, to discuss their work experience and education and seek information about the position.

job market: A market in which employers search for employees and employees search for jobs.

major: The subject or course of study in which a person chooses to earn a degree.

master's degree: A degree that is sought by those who have already earned a bachelor's degree to further their education.

meditation: The practice of focusing the mind for a period of time, sometimes with the aid of chanting.

mental health: A person's health regarding their psychological and emotional well-being.

mindfulness: The practice of focusing awareness on the present moment, while calmly acknowledging and accepting one's feelings, thoughts, and bodily sensations, used as a therapeutic technique.

motivational enhancement therapy (MET): MET typically consists of between two and four treatment sessions and is centered on a counselor prompting motivational statements from the client and supporting this self-motivation.

motivational therapies: Therapies that focus on encouraging a client to find the motivation or drive to overcome a substance addiction.

multidimensional family therapy: Therapy that is geared toward teenagers who abuse substances.

multisystemic family therapy: Therapy focused on helping children and adolescents who have been affected by substance abuse.

music and art therapy: Therapy in which music and art are used to help clients experience, articulate, and engage with emotions.

networking: The processes of building, strengthening, and maintaining professional relationships as a way to further career goals.

nonjudgmental behavior: The ability to observe and accept another without qualifying a behavior as "right" or "wrong."

opioid epidemic: The growing number of deaths and hospitalizations from opioids, including prescriptions, illicit drugs, and analogues.

out-of-state school: A nonprivate college that exists in a state other than in which a person is a resident. These schools have higher tuitions for nonstate residents.

post-traumatic stress disorder (PTSD): A psychiatric disorder that may occur in people who have experienced or witnessed a traumatic event.

private practice: An independent business—include a counseling provider—that is not controlled or paid for by the government or a larger company.

psychology: The scientific study of the human mind and its functions.

résumé: A document, usually one page, that outlines a person's professional experience and education and is designed to give potential employers a sense of a candidate's qualifications.

sober: Without the influence of drugs or alcohol.

sobriety: A state of being sober.

social media: Websites and applications that enable users to create and share content online for networking and social-sharing purposes. Examples include Facebook and Instagram.

sociology: The study of the development, structure, and functioning of human society.

substance abuse: Long-term use or dependence on alcohol or drugs, including daily use, inability to reduce consumption, and negative impacts on social relationships, career, and other areas of function.

substance abuse counselor: A certified, qualified mental health professional specializing in helping people overcome alcohol, drug, and behavioral addictions.

therapy: Treatment for a particular disorder. Therapy can be delivered medicinally or through "talk therapy," in groups or individually.

trauma: An experience that is deeply distressing, physically or emotionally.

treatment facility: A healthcare center that provides counseling and other forms of treatment for substance abuse or mental illnesses.

tuition: The money that is paid for education, be it a university degree or a certification.

twelve-step program: A program led by an organization for the purpose of recovery from substance addictions and behavioral addictions. Alcoholics Anonymous is perhaps the best known.

veteran: A person who has served in a branch of the armed forces.

work culture: A concept that defines the beliefs, philosophy, thought processes, and attitudes of employees in a particular organization.

yoga: A type of exercise in which the body is moved into various positions to become more fit or flexible, to improve breathing, and to relax the mind.

Notes

Introduction

1. Merriam-Webster, "Substance abuse," available at: https://www.merriam-web ster.com/dictionary/substance%20abuse.

2. Merriam-Webster, "Addict," available at: https://www.merriam-webster.com/ dictionary/addict.

3. Addiction Center, "Statistics on Addiction in America," accessed February 15, 2021, at https://www.addictioncenter.com/addiction/addiction-statistics/.

4. David Sparkman, "Drug Abuse on the Rise Because of COVID-19," *EHS Today*, accessed February 15, 2021, at https://www.ehstoday.com/covid19/article/ 21139889/drug-abuse-on-the-rise-because-of-the-coronavirus.

5. Bureau of Labor Statistics, "Substance Abuse, Behavioral Disorder, and Mental Health Counselors," accessed February 15, 2021, at https://www.bls.gov/ooh/community -and-social-service/substance-abuse-behavioral-disorder-and-mental-health-counselors .htm.

Chapter 1

1. Chris Elkins, "Substance Abuse Counselling Techniques," *DrugRehab .com*, accessed February 16, 2021, at https://www.drugrehab.com/treatment/types-of -therapy/.

2. German Lopez, "Why Some People Swear by Alcoholics Anonymous—and Others Despise It," accessed February 16, 2021, at https://www.vox.com/policy-and -politics/2018/1/2/16181734/12-steps-aa-na-studies.

3. Bureau of Labor Statistics, "Substance Abuse, Behavioral Disorder, and Mental Health Counselors," accessed February 16, 2021, at https://www.bls.gov/ooh/community -and-social-service/substance-abuse-behavioral-disorder-and-mental-health-counselors .htm.

4. Walden University, "Why the Demand for Substance Abuse Counselors Continues to Climb," accessed February 16, 2021, at https://www.waldenu.edu/

online-masters-programs/ms-in-clinical-mental-health-counseling/resource/why-the
-demand-for-substance-abuse-counselors-continues-to-climb.

5. David Sparkman, "Drug Abuse on the Rise Because of COVID-19," *EHS Today*, accessed February 16, 2021, at https://www.ehstoday.com/covid19/article/21139889/drug-abuse-on-the-rise-because-of-the-coronavirus.

6. National Institute on Drug Abuse, "Substance Use and Military Life Drug-Facts," accessed February 16, 2021, at https://www.drugabuse.gov/publications/drug facts/substance-use-military-life.

7. AddictionCenter.com, "The Opioid Epidemic," accessed March 2, 2021, at https://www.addictioncenter.com/opiates/opioid-epidemic/.

Chapter 2

1. Irene Shestopal and Jorgen G. Bramness, "Effect of Hypnotherapy in Alcohol Use Disorder Compared to Motivational Interviewing: A Randomised Controlled Trial." *Journal of Addiction Research & Therapy*, Vol 9(5), accessed February 17, 2021, at https://www.omicsonline.org/open-access/effect-of-hypnotherapy-in-alcohol -use-disorder-compared-to-motivational-interviewing-a-randomised-controlled -trial-2155-6105-1000368-105546.html.

2. Careers in Psychology, "Preparing for a Private Counseling Practice," accessed February 17, 2021, at https://careersinpsychology.org/how-prepare-private-counseling -practice/.

Chapter 3

1. Steven R. Antonoff, "College Personality Quiz," *US News and World Report*, accessed October 28, 2020, at https://www.usnews.com/education/best-colleges/right school/choices/articles/college-personality-quiz.

2. Alex Gailey, "Taking a Gap Year During Coronavirus? Here's How to Make the Most of It," *Next Advisor*, accessed October 28, 2020, at https://time.com/next advisor/in-the-news/gap-year-coronavirus/.

3. Claudia Hammond, "Does Reading Fiction Make Us Better People?" *BBC .com*, accessed March 2, 2021, at https://www.bbc.com/future/article/20190523-does -reading-fiction-make-us-better-people.

4. Bureau of Labor Statistics, "How to Become a Substance Abuse, Behavioral Disorder, or Mental Health Counselor," accessed February 22, 2020, at https://www.bls.gov/ooh/community-and-social-service/substance-abuse-behavioral-disorder-and-mental-health-counselors.htm#tab-4.

5. BestColleges.com, "2020 Top Online Addictions Counseling Certificates and Associate Degrees," accessed February 22, 2021, at https://www.bestcolleges.com/features/top-online-substance-abuse-counseling-programs/.

6. CollegeChoice.net, "Best Addiction/Substance Abuse Degrees," accessed February 22, 2021, at https://www.collegechoice.net/rankings/best-addiction-substance-abuse-degrees/.

7. Farran Powell and Emma Kerr, "See the Average College Tuition in 2020–2021," *U.S. News and World Report*, accessed March 2, 2021, at https://www.usnews.com/education/best-colleges/paying-for-college/articles/paying-for-college-infographic.

8. Powell and Kerr, "See the Average College Tuition."

9. Emma Kerr, "How Colleges Are Adjusting Their 2021–2022 Tuition," accessed March 2, 2021, at https://www.usnews.com/education/best-colleges/paying-for-college/articles/how-colleges-are-adjusting-their-2021-2022-tuition.

Chapter 4

1. MyPerfectResume.com, "Substance Abuse Counselor Resume Example + Salaries, Writing Tips and Information," accessed March 2, 2021, at https://www.myperfectresume.com/resume/examples/social-services/substance-abuse-counselor.

2. LiveCareer.com, "Substance Abuse Counselor Resume Examples," accessed March 1, 2021, at https://www.livecareer.com/resume/examples/social-services/substance-abuse-counselor.

3. JobHero.com, "Substance Abuse Counselor Resume Examples," accessed March 2, 2021, at https://www.jobhero.com/resume/examples/social-services/substance-abuse-counselor.

4. The Balance Careers, "Student Resume Examples, Templates, and Writing Tips," accessed February 11, 2020, at https://www.thebalancecareers.com/student-resume-examples-and-templates-2063555.

5. Joshua Waldman, *Job Searching with Social Media For Dummies* (Hoboken, NJ: Wiley & Sons, 2013).

6. SecurityMagazine.com, "70 Percent of Employers Check Candidates' Social Media Profiles," accessed October 30, 2020, at https://www.securitymagazine.com/

articles/89441-percent-of-employers-check-candidates-social-media-profiles#:~:
text=70%20Percent%20Of%20Employers%20Check%20Candidates'%20Social%20
Media%20Profiles,-September%202023%2C%202018&text=According%20to%20
a%20recent%20CareerBuilder,seven%20percent%20plan%20to%20start.

7. Alice E. M. Underwood, "9 Things to Avoid on Social Media While Looking
for a New Job," accessed October 30, 2020, at https://www.glassdoor.com/blog/things
-to-avoid-on-social-media-job-search/.

Bibliography

Addiction Center. "The Opioid Epidemic." Available at: https://www.addiction center.com/opiates/opioid-epidemic/.

———. "Statistics on Addiction in America." Available at: https://www.addictioncenter.com/addiction/addiction-statistics/.

Bureau of Labor Statistics. "How to Become a Substance Abuse, Behavioral Disorder, or Mental Health Counselor." Available at: https://www.bls.gov/ooh/community-and-social-service/substance-abuse-behavioral-disorder-and-mental-health-counselors.htm#tab-4.

———. "Substance Abuse, Behavioral Disorder, and Mental Health Counselors." Available at: https://www.bls.gov/ooh/community-and-social-service/substance-abuse-behavioral-disorder-and-mental-health-counselors.htm.

Careers in Psychology. "Preparing for a Private Counseling Practice." Available at: https://careersinpsychology.org/how-prepare-private-counseling-practice/.

Elkins, Chris. "Substance Abuse Counseling Techniques." *DrugRehab.com*. Available at: https://www.drugrehab.com/treatment/types-of-therapy/.

Hammond, Claudia. "Does reading fiction make us better people?" *BBC.com*. Available at: https://www.bbc.com/future/article/20190523-does-reading-fiction-make-us-better-people.

JobHero.com. "Substance Abuse Counselor Resume Examples." Available at: https://www.jobhero.com/resume/examples/social-services/substance-abuse-counselor.

Kerr, Emma. "How Colleges Are Adjusting Their 2021-2022 Tuition." Available at: https://www.usnews.com/education/best-colleges/paying-for-college/articles/how-colleges-are-adjusting-their-2021-2022-tuition.

LiveCareer.com. "Substance Abuse Counselor Resume Examples." Available at: https://www.livecareer.com/resume/examples/social-services/substance-abuse-counselor.

Lopez, German. "Why Some People Swear by Alcoholics Anonymous—and Others Despise It." Available at: https://www.vox.com/policy-and-politics/2018/1/2/16181734/12-steps-aa-na-studies.

Merriam-Webster. "Substance abuse." Available at: https://www.merriam-webster
.com/dictionary/substance%20abuse.

Merriam-Webster. "Addict." Available at: https://www.merriam-webster.com/
dictionary/addict.

MyPerfectResume.com. "Substance Abuse Counselor Resume Example + Salaries, Writing Tips and Information." Available at: https://www.myperfect
resume.com/resume/examples/social-services/substance-abuse-counselor.

National Institute on Drug Abuse. "Substance Use and Military Life Drug-
Facts." Available at: https://www.drugabuse.gov/publications/drugfacts/
substance-use-military-life.

Powell, Farran, and Emma Kerr. "See the Average College Tuition in 2020-
2021." *U.S. News and World Report.* Available at: https://www.usnews
.com/education/best-colleges/paying-for-college/articles/paying-for-college
-infographic.

Shestopal, Irene, and Jorgen G. Bramness. "Effect of Hypnotherapy in Alcohol Use Disorder Compared to Motivational Interviewing: A Randomised
Controlled Trial." *Journal of Addiction Research & Therapy,* Vol 9(5).
Available at: https://www.omicsonline.org/open-access/effect-of-hypno
therapy-in-alcohol-use-disorder-compared-to-motivational-interviewing
-a-randomised-controlled-trial-2155-6105-1000368-105546.html.

Sparkman, David. "Drug Abuse on the Rise Because of COVID-19." *EHS
Today.* Available at: https://www.ehstoday.com/covid19/article/21139889/
drug-abuse-on-the-rise-because-of-the-coronavirus.

United Nations. "World Drug Report 2019: 35 million people worldwide
suffer from drug use disorders while only 1 in 7 people receive treatment." Available at: https://www.unodc.org/unodc/en/frontpage/2019/
June/world-drug-report-2019_-35-million-people-worldwide-suffer-from
-drug-use-disorders-while-only-1-in-7-people-receive-treatment.html?
ref=fs1.

Walden University. "Why the Demand for Substance Abuse Counselors Continues to Climb." Available at: https://www.waldenu.edu/online-masters
-programs/ms-in-clinical-mental-health-counseling/resource/why-the
-demand-for-substance-abuse-counselors-continues-to-climb.

About the Author

Tracy Brown Hamilton is a writer, editor, and journalist based in the Netherlands. She has written several books on topics ranging from careers to media, economics to pop culture. She lives with her husband and three children.